May I Have Your Attention Please?

Ministering to Those with ADD/ADHD in a Distracted World

Dr. Jason Whitehurst

CROSSBOOKS

CrossBooks™
A Division of LifeWay
1663 Liberty Drive
Bloomington, IN 47403
www.crossbooks.com
Phone: 1-866-879-0502

© 2012 Dr. Jason R. Whitehurst All rights reserved.

No part of this book may be reproduced, stored in a retrieval system, or transmitted by any means without the written permission of the author.

First published by CrossBooks 12/07/2012

ISBN: 978-1-4627-2259-4 (sc)
ISBN: 978-1-4627-2260-0 (e)
ISBN: 978-1-4627-2261-7 (hc)

Printed in the United States of America

Library of Congress Control Number: 2012920318

This book is printed on acid-free paper.

Any people depicted in stock imagery provided by Thinkstock are models, and such images are being used for illustrative purposes only.

Certain stock imagery © Thinkstock.

Because of the dynamic nature of the Internet, any web addresses or links contained in this book may have changed since publication and may no longer be valid. The views expressed in this work are solely those of the author and do not necessarily reflect the views of the publisher, and the publisher hereby disclaims any responsibility for them.

Contents

Introduction ix

Chapter 1—Understanding ADD and ADHD 1

Chapter 2—Creating an Effective Worship Environment for Those with ADD and ADHD 30

Chapter 3—Preaching Effectively to Those with ADD and ADHD 55

Chapter 4—Counseling Effectively Those with ADD and ADHD 81

Chapter 5—Training Volunteers to Work Effectively with Those with ADD and ADHD 98

Appendix A 115

Appendix B 119

Bibliography 139

To my wife and best friend, Maegan. Words cannot describe the effect your constant love and support have had on me. You have helped shape me into the person I am today.

To my precious daughter, Mia. May you grow up to love and serve God all the days of your life. May you understand that if you have initiative, with God as your divine enabler, you can accomplish anything you set your hand to.

Introduction

As churches in America try to stay relevant, church leaders ask questions about how to keep up with culture in a postmodern world. These questions include the following: What is our target audience? Who are we not reaching? Why are we not reaching them? What can we do to stay on the cutting edge of ministry?

Churches that want to create culture will benefit from this book. Churches that wish to communicate the gospel effectively, churches that strive to effectively minister and be on the cutting edge, churches that are always looking to create culture and not just be relevant to it—these churches need to be aware of people in their congregation they may be failing to minister to and help grow spiritually. The congregants I am referring to are those with ADD (attention deficit disorder) or ADHD (attention deficit hyperactivity disorder). The terms ADD and ADHD are often used interchangeably for both those who do and those who do not have symptoms of hyperactivity and impulsiveness.

Several years ago, while serving as a student pastor in North Carolina, I became aware of members of my church who were not being ministered to because I did not have a proper understanding of attention deficit disorder. I was caught up in the same mind-set and view as other pastors and church leaders who were trying to always look outward at whom to minister to, always looking outward to find new people to bring in, and always looking outward to stay culturally relevant. All the while, those who were already in the church and in my group were being neglected because of my lack of understanding and awareness of this real medical condition known as ADD or ADHD.

With this in mind, I embarked on this project to help pastors and church leaders become more effective in their ministry to this special population. It has changed my ministry in a dynamic and positive way. I present this book, hoping that more lives will be changed for the glory of God.

Many ministries pride themselves on being different, being cutting edge. One such ministry is Church Relevant, whose mission statements includes this: "If your ministry is good at the basics—the gospel, the love commandments, and The Great Commission—then holistically studying culture and technology, behavioral science, and best practices for design, leadership, management, marketing, and ministry will only enhance your ministry."[1]

Church Relevant, which is located in my hometown in North Carolina, includes the following statement in its Mission Statement: "Church Relevant is a church that embraces the current culture and uses modern technique to communicate the ancient story."[2] Church Relevant is not an exception but part of the norm. Churches are advertising and promoting themselves as being culturally relevant and openly promoting that they are different from other churches, presenting themselves as churches that can relate and are uniquely different.

Churches that are striving to be culturally relevant are seeking to assimilate and imitate what is going on in the culture of today. In so doing, I believe that many of these churches are losing their effectiveness and are crossing the line from being *in* the world to being *of* the world. As a result, these churches are hard to distinguish from the cultures they are trying to reach.

Churches should not strive to be culturally relevant but rather to engage culture. The apostle Paul addressed this concept in Colossians 4:5–6 (ESV), where he said, "Walk in wisdom toward outsiders, making the best use of the time. Let your speech always be gracious, seasoned with salt, so that you may know how you ought to answer each person." The Bible teaches that Christians are to be engaged with culture. To be engaged with culture means "to participate or be involved in" or "to establish a meaningful connection with."[3]

An example of Christians engaging culture is building relationships and partnering with groups that are not religious. Churches should be involved in the outreach efforts in their community. Nothing speaks to a community more than to see a local church supporting functions and events in the area by volunteering to serve and help other organizations that the church has no affiliation with and that the church is not looking for a kickback from.

If you want your church to engage culture in a powerful way, start doing service evangelism if you are not already. My church donated five thousand hours of community service to our city last year. We went into the community and did service projects throughout the week that not many people would want to do. It was a huge deal, so much so that the local news came and did a piece on what we were doing. We were engaging our local culture through acts of service. This is just one way in which a church can engage culture.

Going a step further, churches should not just be engaging culture but also making culture. In his book, *Culture Making: Recovering Our Creative Calling*, Andy Crouch discusses how Christians should be creating culture. Crouch writes,

Culture is what we make of the world. Culture is, first of all, the name for our relentless, restless human effort to take the world as it's given to us and make something else. This is the original insight of the writer of Genesis when he says that human beings were made in God's image: just like the original Creator, we are creators. God, of course, began with nothing, whereas we begin with something. But the difference is not as great as you might think. For every act of creation involves bringing something into being that was not there before—every creation is ex nihilo, from nothing, even when it takes the world as its starting point.[4]

Crouch's thrust is that the church is not to follow culture or try to be relevant to it but to actually be creators of culture. Crouch cites how Jesus was a creator of culture and not just a passer of it.

Jesus did not simply preserve and pass on His culture's inheritance. Instead, whenever Jesus touched part of Israel's cultural inheritance, He brought something new to it.

Many churches want to be pioneers. They want to be the churches that come up with the newest ministry techniques, the newest way of "doing church." They want to be the church that develops a cutting-edge way of doing ministry. And all the while, they are simply missing out on the opportunity and privilege to minister to a percentage of their people, and they do not even realize it. Just by looking inside the church and being aware of this one issue—congregants with ADD—churches could create culture and see their ministry be revolutionized. But as a general principle, they are too busy looking at those who are not attending rather than those who are.

My goal is elevate the awareness level concerning church members with ADD and to provide insight and practical application into what pastors and church leaders can do to ensure that these congregants are not being neglected. There needs to be an understanding that those with ADD or ADHD are sitting in church services each and every week and never really growing spiritually because those over them in the Lord are simply not dialed in to the fact that they are not ministering to them because of their condition.

This book will serve as a guide or manual to inform and educate pastors and church leaders about the nature of the disease, what it is, how it is treated medically, and practical ways to increase the effectiveness of churches in their ministry to their parishioners who have this medical malady. It is my passion and desire that this project will be beneficial in equipping and empowering pastors and church leaders. I pray that the knowledge and information presented would fall on eager hearts and open minds, so that the kingdom of God would be edified and that a multitude of church members across America who suffer from ADD or ADHD would be ministered to in a way that they never have before. Spiritual growth and maturity would follow.

Endnotes:

1. "About - churchrelevance.com." Church Relevance. http://churchrelevance.com/about/ (accessed April 2, 2012).
2. "CR Mission Church Relevant – New Bern, NC." Church Relevant – New Bern, NC. http://churchrelevant.com/cr-mission/ (accessed April 3, 2012).
3. Morrow, Think Christianly: Looking at the Intersection of Faith and Culture, 41.
4. Andy Crouch, Culture Making: Recovering Our Creative Calling (Downers Grove, IL: IVP Books, 2008). Kindle Electronic Edition: Chapter 1, location 189.

Chapter 1
Understanding ADD and ADHD

Knowledge is power. People cannot treat what they do not understand. A pastor, minister, or lay leader cannot effectively minister to someone with ADD or ADHD if he does not have a fundamental grasp and knowledge of the disease. The more thorough the level of knowledge and understanding, the more effective the pastor, minister, or church leader will be in dealing with those who are diagnosed with the disease.

I have met countless pastors and ministers who had no clue about ADD or ADHD and how it affected their members. The major obstacle is that most people, including doctors, do not know much about the condition, nor do they know how to diagnose it or treat it, according to Dr. Lenard Adler who is the director of the Adult ADHD program at the NYU School of Medicine.[5]

Another noteworthy clinician, Dr. Hallowell, who was a professor at Harvard University and now is the head of the Hallowell Center for Cognitive and Emotional Health in Massachusetts, said, "Most doctors don't know much about ADD, and few teachers knew about it when you were in school. Back then people just dismissed you as stupid or just bad."[6]

Adler also cites a patient who writes, "I just wish the average adult knew about this condition, and I wish the facts were more widely understood."[7] Many patients feel that people in general just do not understand ADD and ADHD. Patients wish more people understood the difficulties of living with such a hindering disease and not diminishing how real the disease is. The words that ADD and ADHD patients hear are, "Why don't you just pay attention?" or "Snap out of it." If only it was that simple. Saying to an ADD or ADHD sufferer to "just snap out of it and pay attention" is akin to saying to a crippled person, "Why don't you just get up and walk out of here?"

Adler says that he gets literally tens of thousands of similar messages from people who feel the same way. From reading these statements, obviously there is a recognizable lack of understanding and knowledge of the disease with many Americans. To reiterate, these noteworthy experts are saying that their colleagues in the medical field do not really know much about the disease, as a general rule.

I have spoken with many pastors and church leaders who simply think that someone who claims to have ADD or ADHD is just using it as an excuse not to pay attention, or that it is just an attempt by doctors and those in the medical field to justify irrational behavior. Clearly, this is not the case. ADD and ADHD are real medical issues, which science solidifies.

May I Have Your Attention Please?

Pastors, ministers, and church leaders need to have knowledge and understanding of ADD and ADHD. If one were to ask why it is important for them to know, the answer to that question is simple: pastors, ministers, and church leaders are called to a higher calling and should strive to ever be learning so that they may be even more effective in their respective ministries.

The Bible records in 2 Timothy 2:15 (KJV), "Study to shew thyself approved unto God, a workman that needeth not to be ashamed, rightly dividing the word of truth." The exhortation is presented: the principle to constantly be learning and studying and gleaning things to improve as a pastor or minister. The application obviously applies to the Word of God, but the breadth of the application stretches farther into today's culture in which so much can be learned to make a pastor more successful and effective.

Also, the Bible records in Luke 12:48b (NASB), "From everyone who has been given much, much will be required; and to whom they entrusted much, of him they will ask all the more." Pastors and ministers have been given a great responsibility by being entrusted with the spiritual well-being of those that God has placed under them in their care. That includes those who have ADD. Therefore, there is a burden on pastors seen in the Scriptures to be diligent in gaining knowledge in every area they can, which will make them more effective for the kingdom of God and shepherding His people.

People in congregations who have the disease are not being ministered to as much as they could be, and it is because their leaders do not understand. And maybe it is because they do not care to understand, or maybe they never considered the topic before, the disease itself. The saying is, "You cannot rise higher than the platform," which means if the one in charge of leading in the front of the church does not understand the disease, how it works, whom it affects, and what all it entails, then nothing is going to be done to minister to those who have it.

The condemning challenges faced by people in church with ADD or ADHD, particularly those not yet diagnosed, must be horrific. The church social environment leans strongly toward interpreting behavior through a moral prism. In ignorance, pastors and church leaders most likely will identify a person with AD/HD as having profound Christian character issues, offer counsel to repent, and then react negatively when no real change is observed over even a long period.[8]

The problem is only getting worse. Statistics show a rise in the number of ADD and ADHD diagnoses.[9] Each year, more and more people are diagnosed. As the amount of children and adults being diagnosed with the disease increases, the more clear it becomes that there needs to be awareness, education, and a guide on how to effectively minister to those affected by the disease.

My hope is that this chapter will provide what many people, including doctors, lack, which is an effective and thorough understanding of ADD or ADHD. The data and information presented is the latest medical and scientific data that has been published by leaders and pioneers in the field of studying ADD and ADHD.

Defining ADD and ADHD

To begin to understand ADD and ADHD, they must be defined as to what real ADD is, and also what the disease is not. There are many myths and misconceptions about the disease, which will be discussed later in the chapter. Therefore, it is important to establish medical and scientific definitions of the disease.

The diagnostic manual of mental health problems, called the DSM-IV, defines ADD by a set of eighteen symptoms, which will be discussed later in the chapter. To qualify for the diagnosis, you need six. These symptoms only emphasize the downside of ADD, or the negative aspects of the disease, and do not note the positive symptoms.[10]

Attention deficit disorder is a general term frequently used to describe individuals that have attention deficit hyperactivity disorder without the hyperactive and impulsive behaviors. ADD is the old term that clinicians used, and it has been replaced by many with ADHD. For the purpose of this book, the words will be used interchangeably as not to confuse to the reader.

Attention deficit hyperactivity disorder is the official name used by the American Psychiatric Association, and it encompasses hyperactive, impulsive, and/or inattentive behaviors.[11] ADHD is a problem with inattentiveness, overactivity, impulsivity, or a combination. For these problems to be diagnosed as ADHD, they must be out of the normal range.[12]

ADHD is one of the most common neurobehavioral disorders of childhood. It is usually first diagnosed in childhood and often lasts into adulthood.[13] There are three different types of ADHD, and the type depends on the strength of the symptoms in each person. The three types are

1. **Predominantly Inattentive Type:** It is hard for the individual to organize or finish a task, to pay attention to details, or to follow instructions or conversations. The person is easily distracted or forgets details of daily routines.

2. **Predominantly Hyperactive-Impulsive Type:** The person fidgets and talks a lot. It is hard to sit still for long (e.g., for a meal or while doing homework). Smaller children may run, jump, or climb constantly. The individual feels restless and has trouble with impulsivity. Someone who is impulsive may interrupt others a lot, grab things from people, or speak at inappropriate times. It is hard for the person to wait his or her turn or listen to directions. A person with impulsiveness may have more accidents and injuries than others.

3. **Combined Type:** Symptoms of the above two types are equally present in the person.

With a proper understanding of the medical definition of ADD or ADHD, what ADD and ADHD are not can be better understood. Many tendencies and behaviors exhibited in people with ADD also appear in people that do not have the disease. The manifestation of one or another of these traits is not unusual but actually common. In fact, almost every person on the earth at one time or another has displayed most of the behaviors associated with ADD.[14]

ADD is not simply having some of the symptoms associated with the disease. What determines whether or not it is ADD is the total picture of a person's state and actions, his intertwined existences, intensities of behavior, and frequencies.

Symptoms of ADD

The very definitions of ADD and ADHD illustrate a couple of the symptoms. There are more symptoms listed that need to be understood that go beyond just the inability to pay attention or hyperactivity.

Many times a doctor or person is quick to make judgment about a disease because the sufferer has a symptom or two that relates to the disease. For example, just because a person is very particular and does something the same way over and over does, it not mean that person has obsessive-compulsive disorder. Or just because a person experiences a period of grief along with apathy and has no interest in doing anything, it does not mean that that person is in a clinical depression. Often, doctors are quick to make diagnoses. More symptoms need to be examined that pertain to ADD and ADHD to get a better understanding of all the potential symptoms.

I've learned that those who suffer from ADD and ADHD sit in church services each week but do not get as much as they could out of the service. One must look no farther than the symptoms for diagnosing ADD and ADHD to understand why.

ADD is defined by the presence or absence of the symptoms set forth in the DSM-IV. The symptoms fall into three categories: lack of attention (inattentiveness), hyperactivity, and impulsive behavior (impulsivity).[15]

There are two clusters of symptoms, one describing symptoms of inattention and the other cluster describing symptoms of hyperactivity and impulsivity. To be even considered for a diagnosis, the criteria set forth in cluster 1 and cluster 2 must be met.[16]

In cluster 1, six or more of the following symptoms of inattention have to persist for at least six months to a degree that is maladaptive and inconsistent with a developmental level:[17]

Inattention

1. Often fails to give close attention to details or makes careless mistakes in schoolwork, work, or other activities

2. Often has difficulty sustaining attention in tasks or play activities

3. Often does not seem to listen when spoken to directly

4. Often does not follow through on instructions and fails to finish schoolwork, chores, or duties in the workplace (not due to oppositional failure or failure to understand instructions)

5. Often has difficulty organizing tasks and activities

6. Often avoids, dislikes, or is reluctant to engage in tasks that require sustained mental effort

7. Often loses things necessary for tasks or activities

8. Is often easily distracted by extraneous stimuli

9. Is often forgetful in daily activities

In cluster 2, six or more of the following symptoms of hyperactivity and impulsivity have persisted for at least six months to a degree that is maladaptive and inconsistent with developmental level:[18]

Hyperactivity

1. Often fidgets with hands or feet or squirms in seat

2. Often leaves seat in classroom or other situations in which remaining seated is expected

3. Often runs about or climbs excessively when it is inappropriate (in adolescents and adults, may be limited to subjective feelings of restlessness)

4. Often has difficulty playing or engaging in leisure activities quietly

5. Is often "on the go" or acts as if "driven by a motor"

6. Often talks excessively

Impulsivity

7. Often blurts out answers before questions have been completed

8. Often has difficulty awaiting his or her turn

9. Often interrupts or intrudes on others

The following behaviors and problems may stem directly from ADHD or may be the result of related adjustment difficulties:[19]

1. Chronic lateness and forgetfulness

2. Anxiety

3. Low self-esteem

4. Employment problems

5. Difficulty controlling anger

6. Impulsiveness

7. Substance abuse or addiction

8. Poor organization skills

9. Procrastination

10. Low frustration tolerance

11. Chronic boredom

12. Difficulty concentrating when reading

13. Mood swings

14. Depression

15. Relationship problems

There are also other symptoms related to adults with ADD or ADHD. Adults with ADD may have had a history of poorer educational performance and were underachievers by normal educational standards. They likely have had more frequent school disciplinary actions. They may have had to repeat a grade.

Adults with ADD are shown to have dropped out of school more often. Adults are more likely to change employers more frequently. They are more likely to belong to a lower income class. They may have more driving violations because their inability to focus or hyperactivity. They are more likely to abuse illegal substances. They are more likely to end up in divorce. All of these symptoms are more likely in adults with ADHD.[20]

Just looking at the cluster lists, many people would identify with the symptoms on any given day. If one looks at them individually or several of them together, one recognizes a symptom or several symptoms in one's own actions and behavior. Yet that is not enough to diagnose with ADD. The bottom line is most, if not all, people have symptoms of ADD, but not everyone is diagnosed with the disease.

Diagnosis of ADD and ADHD

Like other disorders and illnesses, ADHD can be difficult for a clinical practitioner to diagnose. The reason is because there are no definitive biological indicators, such as elevated levels of glucose in the blood or urine to suggest the presence of ADD. Many people argue that there is an overdiagnosis of ADD and ADHD in children. I believe part of the reason is the consistent rise in diagnoses every year. I would say to those who argue that there is an overdiagnosis that doctors do the best they can with the diagnosing criteria to make an accurate assessment. It has been my experience that those people I know who have been diagnosed were legitimately diagnosed based on the symptoms set forth. I personally believe there is likely an underdiagnosis, especially in older teens and young adults.

A positive diagnosis of ADD or ADHD is based on a doctor's ability to recognize the symptoms present, to ascertain and determine the severity and frequency of the symptoms, to qualify the impact the symptoms are having on the person's life, and to verify that the onset of symptoms occurred during childhood through a series of interviews and evaluations.[21]

Even though diagnosis is somewhat tricky, there is a general guideline by which ADD is diagnosed. Referring to the cluster of symptoms in the previous section, a patient must have six out of nine symptoms in either cluster to be diagnosed with ADD or ADHD.[22] Also in adults, the onset of symptoms must date back to

May I Have Your Attention Please?

childhood, middle school, or before. There is no such thing as adult onset ADD.[23]

Deciding if a child has ADHD is a several-step process. There is no single test to diagnose ADHD, and many other problems, like anxiety, depression, and certain types of learning disabilities, can have similar symptoms. One step of the process involves having a medical exam, including hearing and vision tests, to rule out other problems. Another part of the process may include a checklist for rating ADHD symptoms and taking a history of the child from parents, teachers, and sometimes the child.[24]

Too often, difficult children are incorrectly labeled with ADHD. On the other hand, many children who do have ADHD remain undiagnosed. In either case, related learning disabilities or mood problems are often missed. The American Academy of Pediatrics has issued guidelines to bring more clarity to this issue. The diagnosis is based on very specific symptoms, which must be present in more than one setting.

- Children should have at least six attention symptoms or six hyperactivity/impulsivity symptoms, with some symptoms present before age seven.

- The symptoms must be present for at least six months, seen in two or more settings, and not caused by another problem.

- The symptoms must be severe enough to cause significant difficulties in many settings, including home, school, and relationships with peers.[25]

Various professionals are qualified to diagnose ADD. Child psychiatrists and developmental pediatricians have the most training in this area. Child psychiatrists diagnose and treat both children and adults with ADD, while developmental pediatricians only deal with children.[26]

The diagnosis of ADD in children and adults really boils down to four things. First, what are the nature, frequency, and severity of the symptoms? Second, if the symptoms presented themselves in childhood. Third, how chronic and pervasive the symptoms are. And fourth, how much do the symptoms interfere with the everyday life of the patient?[27] If these four criteria are examined and determined to be true and evident, then a diagnosis can follow.

A problem that many doctors and clinicians have is the amount of patients who are misdiagnosed and the amount of patients who go undiagnosed. It bears repeating that diagnosing ADD or ADHD is not an exact science. It is based on the most up-to-date medical and scientific information available, but doctors do not always get it right. The most effective measure for diagnosing ADD is an intensive evaluation and interview.[28]

It is important for pastors and church leaders to understand just because a doctor has diagnosed a church member with ADD or ADHD, it does not authenticate that the disease is real in that person's life. There can be a misdiagnosis. And conversely, just because

May I Have Your Attention Please?

a church member does not have a doctor that has diagnosed them with ADD or ADHD, it does not mean he or she does not have the disease. That is why it is imperative that pastors, ministers, and church leaders are educated and effectively understand the disease and all in entails.

The more knowledge the pastor or minister or church leader has of ADD or ADHD, the more he possibly can see about the church member that a doctor may not see. Because a pastor or church leader may have more contact with a parishioner than a doctor would, a pastor or minister is not a medical doctor and cannot diagnose ADD but he can recognize the symptoms and draw a potential inference that a diagnosis is legit or not legit. If the pastor or church leader has a good relationship with the church member and feels comfortable, he may desire to discuss the diagnosis or lack thereof in an effort to help the person get treatment if needed.

Statistics on ADD and ADHD

In understanding ADD, it is noteworthy to have knowledge of the numbers behind the disease. ADHD is more common than doctors may have previously believed, according to a new study from the Mayo Clinic.[29] Roughly 5 to 8 percent of Americans have been diagnosed with ADD.[30] ADD or ADHD is one of the best-documented developmental problems in children. The American Psychiatric Association states in *Diagnostic and Statistical Manual of Mental Disorders* (DSM-IV-TR) that 3 percent to 7 percent of school-aged children have ADHD.[31] It is now known that these symptoms continue into adulthood for about 60 percent of children with ADHD. That translates into 4 percent of the US adult population, or eight million adults.[32] However, most of the adults who have ADD or ADHD do not realize it because they have never been diagnosed with it. Few adults are identified or treated for the disease.[33]

The latest statistics from the Centers for Disease Control and Prevention as of the time of this project are the following:[34]

- Number of children 3–17 years of age ever diagnosed with ADHD: 5.2 million

- Percent of children 3–17 years of age ever diagnosed with ADHD: 8.4 percent

- Percent of boys 3–17 years of age ever diagnosed with ADHD: 11.2 percent

- Percent of girls 3–17 years of age ever diagnosed with ADHD 5.5 percent

It is known that adults do have ADD. Studies into adult ADD began in the late 1970s. At one time, it was considered a children's disease, but as information increases about the disease, the more that is known concerning adult ADD. Of the roughly ten million adults with ADD, only about 15 percent are identified and treated.[35] ADHD afflicts approximately 3 percent to 10 percent of school-aged children and an estimated 60 percent of those will maintain the disorder into adulthood.[36]

May I Have Your Attention Please?

The numbers do not lie. There has been a steady increase in the number of diagnoses since 2003. Dr. Russell Barkley has compiled the following statistics concerning ADHD:

- A classroom with thirty students will have between one and three children with ADHD.

- Boys are diagnosed with ADHD three times more often than girls. (I have seen no research or studies to indicate a reason for this.)

- Emotional development in children with ADHD is 30 percent slower than in their non-ADD peers. This means that a child that is ten years old will have the emotional development of a seven-year-old and a twenty-year-old will have the emotional maturity of a fourteen-year-old.

- One fourth of children with ADHD have serious learning disabilities, such as oral expression, listening skills, reading comprehension, and/or math.

- 65 percent of children with ADHD exhibit problems in defiance or problems with authority figures. This can include verbal hostility and temper tantrums.

- 75 percent of boys diagnosed with ADD/ADHD have hyperactivity.

- 60 percent of girls diagnosed with ADD/ADHD have hyperactivity.

- 50 percent of children with ADHD experience sleep problems.

- Teenagers with ADHD have almost four times as many traffic citations as non-ADD/ADHD drivers. They have four times as many car accidents and are seven times more likely to have a second accident.

- 21 percent of teens with ADHD skip school on a regular basis, and 35 percent drop out of school before finishing high school.

- 45 percent of children with ADHD have been suspended from school at least once.

- 30 percent of children with ADHD have repeated a year in school.[37]

The statistics are sobering. These children grow up to be adults, and as the numbers show, ADD carries over into adulthood for a majority of those who have the disease. These children will soon be in the sanctuaries of America, and pastors, ministers, and church leaders have to be painfully aware of the landscape surrounding the disease and how it affects their ministry in the local church.

Causes of ADD and ADHD

Before discussing the causes for the disease, it should first be pointed out that there is no way to stop a person from having the disease once he or she is born. Although there is no proven way to prevent ADHD, early identification and treatment can prevent many of the problems associated with ADHD.[38]

The basis for ADD or ADHD is mostly biological, with heredity contributing about 75 percent of the causal factors.[39] The cause is not behavioral in the sense that someone with ADD chooses to act a certain way. Rather, that person is compelled to respond a certain way in a given situation. It may appear on the outside as if he has a choice, but physiologically he does not. What goes on in his brain prompts him to a certain response.[40]

This is welcome news to many, that ADD is a biological condition many times and is determined by the genes of the parents before birth. These genes are passed down from generation to generation. It does not mean that just because a parent has ADD or ADHD that it will be passed to the child. If both parents have ADHD, the child is more likely to have the genetic predisposition.[41] The factors present for ADD exist in the brain prior to the child entering the world.[42]

ADHD appears related to two neurotransmitters: dopamine and norepinephrine. Neurotransmitters are used by the brain to stimulate or repress stimulation in brain cells. To pay proper attention, the brain must be adequately stimulated. To have proper control of our impulses, areas of the brain must be adequately controlled, repressed, or slowed down. In ADHD children, both systems of stimulation and repression are not working correctly. Some studies suggest that ADHD children/adults may have only 10 to 25 percent of these two neurotransmitters found in the normal brain.[43]

Inattention and distractibility appear to be related to low levels of norepinephrine. ADHD children/adults can't judge which things in their environment are important and which should be ignored. ADHD children/adults often feel the flight path of a fly in the room is as important as the teacher's algebra lesson. To the ADHD child or adult, everything on the desk is equally interesting and worthy of attention. Low levels of norepinephrine also make it very difficult for ADHD children and adults to sustain their focus on a task, plan ahead, and understand such concepts as sequence and time.[44]

There are nongenetic factors that can increase the likelihood of a child being born with ADD. Substances taken in by the mother during pregnancy can alter cells in the fetus. A mother who smokes, drinks, or abuses drugs may be putting her unborn child at risk for ADHD. The evidence for this conclusion is mounting.[45]

In addition to genetics, scientists are studying other possible causes and risk factors including, brain injury, environmental exposures (e.g., lead), premature delivery, and low birth weight.[46] Research does not support the popularly held views that ADHD is caused by eating too much sugar, watching too much television, parenting, or social and environmental factors, such as poverty or family chaos.

May I Have Your Attention Please?

Treatments for ADD and ADHD

The best treatment for ADD is a combination of medication and behavior therapy. Some of the commonly prescribed medications are Adderall, Concerta, Dexedrine, Ritalin, and Focalin. All of these medications are psychostimulants. There are some prescribed medications that are not stimulants, such as Strattera and Intuniv. These nonstimulants are prescribed when the side effects of the stimulant medications are too much to bear. There is no one treatment that will work for every person diagnosed with ADD. It is much more effective to combine treatments than to rely on a single source to treat the disease.

The goal of treating adults with ADD is different from the goal of treating children. For adults, a treatment is needed that will last throughout the day, as adults are busy with work and other activities. For children, medication can be given by a school nurse at intervals; therefore, the treatment does not have to be stretched out across the day.

The best protocol for treatment combinations is based on variables, such as the type of ADD or ADHD the patient has, the symptoms the patient is experiencing, optimizing the length of treatment throughout the day, whether or not the patient has other medications or conditions that need to be considered, and perceptions about the medication available to ADD sufferers.

Coexisting conditions can make treating a patient with ADD difficult. For example, if a patient has been diagnosed with clinical depression or bipolar disorder, or any other condition, a physician must make sure each condition is treated and not just one treatment for all of the conditions. Having coexisting conditions in patients with ADD is not the exception; it is the norm.[47] Oftentimes, a doctor will prescribe more than one medication just for the ADD, especially in adults whose lives are busier and more complex. Physicians really need to be aware of all the conditions and issues going on with their patients, or one of the coexisting conditions will not get treated.

Cognitive behavioral therapy is another form of treatment for those suffering from ADD. It is a combination of two different kinds of therapy: cognitive therapy and behavior therapy. The cognitive therapy focuses on showing the patient how thinking patterns can be the cause of unwanted symptoms that go along with their ADD. Behavior therapy shows the patient how to be strong when faced with impulses to act a certain way in a given situation. This treatment helps ADD patients take control of their thoughts and behave in a way that is rational and with a clear mind.

Coaching is a treatment that is growing in popularity, likely due to its effectiveness. With this type of treatment, there is a coach-patient relationship in which the coach helps the patient set goals and obtain objectives. Many ADD patients like the one-on-one coaching and feel it is more effective for them as a treatment option.

The best treatment is a combination of medicine and either cognitive behavioral therapy or coaching. Any time more than one treatment is applied at working against a disease or condition, the results are usually dramatically better and quicker than a stand-alone method of treatment. ADD is the same way. Patients with combined treatments see better results than if they were to just go with one of the treatment options solo.

Myths and Misconceptions about ADD and ADHD

The first myth is that everyone has the symptoms of ADD, and that anyone with average intelligence can overcome these symptoms. The truth is that ADD affects all levels of intelligence. And it is true that many, if not all, people exhibit certain symptoms of ADD, but only those chronic impairments warrant an ADD diagnosis.[48] This is important: ADD is not normal inattention. It is much more severe, it is a chronic problem and not just a bad day focusing.

Another myth is that ADD is a simple problem of being hyperactive or not listening when someone is talking to you. The truth is ADD is a complex disorder that involves impairments in focus, organization, motivation, emotional modulation, memory, and other functions of the brain's management system.[49] There is nothing simple or elementary about the disease. This myth is used by those who would like to easily dismiss ADD as problem that someone can just get over or snap out of. It isn't simple at all; it is complex. Any time a disease affects brain chemicals, it is usually fairly complex.

A third myth is that ADD is a childhood problem that doesn't affect adults. The general public truly believes this.[50] The truth is that adults suffer from the disease as well. ADD does not just affect children, which is why it is important that pastors and ministers understand the disease, because every Sunday and during the week they deal with adults who have the disease, whether it is diagnosed or not. Terms like *lazy* and *incompetent* are used to describe these adults, in what is referred to as a "moral diagnosis." When we morally judge these adults, they experience feelings of despair, ineptitude, and hopelessness more deeply.

To show how dangerous a moral diagnosis can be, some adults feel so bad that they resort to drug abuse, violent crimes, and reckless and dangerous behavior.[51] This does not have to be so. If the myth is dispelled, it would change the lives of many adults. Pastors and ministers must understand ADD and ADHD are not just a kid's disease. They are prevalent among adults.

A fourth myth is that ADD is just a lack of willpower, that people with ADD focus on things that interest them, and that they could focus on other tasks if they really wanted to. The truth is that ADD has nothing to do with willpower, even though it may appear that way. ADD is a brain-chemical problem.[52] I know this is being redundant, but telling someone who has ADD to "just pay attention" or to "just calm down" would be like saying to a paralytic "just get up and walk." It is not a matter of willpower or wanting to. Pastors and ministers who get frustrated with ADD congregants, because they are not paying attention or seem to be antsy or have hyperactivity, must understand that it is not intentional; if the person could do something about it, he or she most likely would. They are compelled to act that way because their brains are not functioning like a normal human being's brain.

Finally, there is the myth that ADD does not really affect someone's life, the myth that ADD does not really cause damage

May I Have Your Attention Please?

to how a person lives. The truth is, and hopefully it is evident by now, this is utterly false. Untreated or inadequately treated ADD can impair learning, family life, education, work life, social interactions, and driving safety.[53] All one has to do is ask ADD sufferers what ADD has done to their lives, the lifestyle changes they have had to make, how it has impaired things many people take for granted, and the truth will be evident.

Endnotes:

1. Lenard Adler and Mari Florence, Scattered Minds: Hope and Help for Adults with Attention Deficit Hyperactivity Disorder (New York: G. P. Putnam's Sons, 2006), xii.
2. Edward M. Hallowell and John J. Ratey, Delivered from Distraction: Getting the Most out of Life with Attention Deficit Disorder (New York, NY: Ballantine Books, 2006), xxviii.
3. Ibid., xi.
4. Jonathan Scott Halverstadt and Jerry Seiden, ADD, Christianity & the Church: A Compassionate Healing Resource to Inform, Inspire, & Illuminate, by Janet. Goodreads.com Book Review, August 20, 2010.
5. "CDC - ADHD, Data and Statistics - NCBDDD." Centers for Disease Control and Prevention. http://www.cdc.gov/ncbddd/adhd/data.html (accessed April 1, 2012).
6. Hallowell and Ratey, Delivered from Distraction, 4.
7. Ibid.
8. "Attention Deficit Hyperactivity Disorder (ADHD): MedlinePlus Medical Encyclopedia." National Library of Medicine - National Institutes of Health. http://www.nlm.nih.gov/medlineplus/ency/article/001551.htm (accessed April 1, 2012).
9. "CDC - ADHD, Facts - NCBDDD." Centers for Disease Control and Prevention. http://www.cdc.gov/ncbddd/adhd/facts.html (accessed April 3, 2012).
10. Adler and Florence, Scattered Minds, 60.

11. "Attention Deficit Hyperactivity Disorder (ADHD): MedlinePlus Medical Encyclopedia." National Library of Medicine - National Institutes of Health. http://www.nlm.nih.gov/medlineplus/ency/article/001551.htm (accessed April 1, 2012).
12. Hallowell and Ratey, Delivered from Distraction, 118.
13. Ibid.
14. Ibid., 119.
15. "ADHD in Adults: Symptoms, Statistics, Causes, Types, Treatments, and More." WebMD - Better information. Better health. http://www.webmd.com/add-adhd/guide/adhd-adults (accessed April 1, 2012).
16. Ibid.
17. Adler and Florence, Scattered Minds, 91.
18. Hallowell and Ratey, Delivered from Distraction, 119.
19. Ibid.
20. "CDC - ADHD, Facts - NCBDDD." Centers for Disease Control and Prevention. http://www.cdc.gov/ncbddd/adhd/facts.html (accessed April 3, 2012).
21. "Attention Deficit Hyperactivity Disorder (ADHD): MedlinePlus Medical Encyclopedia." National Library of Medicine - National Institutes of Health. http://www.nlm.nih.gov/medlineplus/ency/article/001551.htm (accessed April 1, 2012).
22. Hallowell and Ratey, Delivered from Distraction, 117.
23. Adler and Florence, Scattered Minds, 100.
24. Thomas E. Brown, Attention Deficit Disorder: The Unfocused Mind in Children and Adults (New Haven, CT: Yale University Press, 2006), 167.
25. "Statistics about ADD in Adults & Children ADDitude - Adults & Children with ADD ADHD." Attention Deficit Disorder ADHD Symptoms, Medication, Treatment, Diagnosis, Parenting ADD Children and More: Information from ADDitude. http://www.

additudemag.com/adhd/article/688.html (accessed April 1, 2012).

26. Hallowell and Ratey, Delivered from Distraction, 8.
27. "CDC - ADHD, Data and Statistics - NCBDDD." Centers for Disease Control and Prevention. http://www.cdc.gov/ncbddd/adhd/data.html (accessed April 1, 2012).
28. "ADHD in Adults: Symptoms, Statistics, Causes, Types, Treatments, and More." WebMD - Better information. Better health. http://www.webmd.com/add-adhd/guide/adhd-adults (accessed April 1, 2012).
29. Ibid.
30. "FASTSTATS - Attention Deficit Hyperactivity Disorder." Centers for Disease Control and Prevention. http://www.cdc.gov/nchs/fastats/adhd.htm (accessed April 1, 2012).
31. Hallowell and Ratey, Delivered from Distraction, 8.
32. "ADHD in Adults: Symptoms, Statistics, Causes, Types, Treatments, and More." WebMD - Better information. Better health. http://www.webmd.com/add-adhd/guide/adhd-adults (accessed April 1, 2012).
33. "ADD/ADHD Statistics - What Is ADHD? - ADHD." HealthCentral.com - Trusted, Reliable and Up To Date Health Information. http://www.healthcentral.com/adhd/c/1443/13716/addadhd-statistics (accessed April 1, 2012).
34. "Attention Deficit Hyperactivity Disorder (ADHD): MedlinePlus Medical Encyclopedia." National Library of Medicine - National Institutes of Health. http://www.nlm.nih.gov/medlineplus/ency/article/001551.htm (accessed April 1, 2012).
35. Adler and Florence, Scattered Minds, 75.
36. Ibid.
37. Ibid., 80.
38. Ibid., 76.

39. "Attention-Deficit Hyperactivity Disorder (ADHD)." Joseph M Carver, PhD - Clinical Psychologist. http://www.drjoecarver.com/clients/49355/File/Attention-Deficit%20Hyperactivity%20Disorder%20(ADHD).html (accessed April 5, 2012).
40. Ibid.
41. Ibid., 81.
42. "CDC - ADHD, Facts - NCBDDD." Centers for Disease Control and Prevention. http://www.cdc.gov/ncbddd/adhd/facts.html (accessed April 3, 2012).
43. Ibid., 120.
44. Brown, Attention Deficit Disorder, 167.
45. Ibid., 20.
46. Adler and Florence, Scattered Minds, xi.
47. Ibid., xii.
48. Brown, Attention Deficit Disorder, 1.
49. Ibid., 296.

Chapter 2

Creating an Effective Worship Environment for Those with ADD and ADHD

Worship services are not always known as the most exciting hour of the week for most churchgoers. Many people attend church out of a sense of obligation or duty rather than the joy they feel by attending a service or the sense of spiritual renewal or awakening they might receive. I've found the vast majority of churchgoers do not have a deep yearning to be in church to worship a holy and righteous God. They are there out of tradition or force of habit. It's just what they do on Sunday mornings.

If you ask them, "How was the church service today?" they reply, "It was okay." If you ask them if they enjoyed the music, they might reply, "It was all right." You may ask them if they enjoyed the sermon, and they might reply, "Sure, it was pretty good." The question that needs to be asked is, "Shouldn't the church worship experience be just that, an experience?" For most church attendees, has the church worship service become just okay or all right or pretty good? What

May I Have Your Attention Please?

has changed in the world that so many Sunday morning attendees do not get anything out of the hour to the hour and a half they spend in the house of God?

Based on my experience—talking with churchgoers over the last fifteen years, studying church-growth techniques, and attending church-growth conferences—the answer is that society and culture have changed. This is the age of postmodernism and churches are striving to remain relevant and effective in the midst of a culture that is rapidly changing in ideology, technology, and worldviews. As seen in the last chapter, the number of ADD diagnoses continues to increase, and many churches have not adapted to meet the needs of these congregants.

If people who do not have ADD or ADHD walk out and can't remember much about the worship service because they were not engaged in it or because it was just "okay," then what chance do people with ADD or ADHD have of gaining anything meaningful out of the same service? Thirty minutes after the service, everyone should be able to recall the songs that were sung, the message that was preached, and the announcements that were made. Knowing the symptoms of ADD as established in the last chapters, such as inattentiveness, hyperactivity, and being easily distracted, it would seem obvious that that particular worship service was not structured in a way for it to be a worship experience.

In order to minister to ADD congregants on a Sunday morning or whenever a worship service is held, it must be effectively created to overcome the obstacles they face because of their disease, so that they are ministered to and leave the worship service spiritually renewed and quenched in their thirst for an encounter or experience with God. After all, is that not what God created man for, to worship God and experience Him in all of His glory?

The Importance of Creating the Environment

It is imperative that a worship environment is created with ADD or ADHD congregants in mind. If a pastor or minister were to follow this logic, it makes sense: if a worship service is created and structured in a way to minister to those with ADD, then would not the rest of the congregation also benefit from the structure and elements in place? Put more simply, if those with ADD glean something from a worship service, doesn't it make sense that everyone else would too?

Worship is a face-to-face encounter with the living God, based on a regeneration experience, prompted by the Holy Spirit, and resulting in exhortation of God's glory.[54] Since worship is giving all of our praise to God with all of our hearts, worship is an intense emotional, intellectual, and volitional response to the majesty of God.[55] Worship is an experience that is meant to be partaken in by the people of God. That is why pastors, ministers, and church leaders must be expedient and proactive about producing a worship service environment that is conducive for true, genuine worship to take place for those with ADD or ADHD.

There is a difference between true worship and activities that take place in a church but are not true worship; they may even be considered anti-worship. Jesus talked about true worship in John 4:23–24 when He said, "But the hour is coming, and is now here, when the true worshipers will worship the Father in spirit and truth, for the Father is seeking such people to worship him. God is spirit, and those who worship him must worship in spirit and truth" (ESV).

Worship is a face-to-face relationship with God. Six elements should occur in all true worship: examination, expectation, appropriation, meditation, consummation, and transformation.[56]

Examination worship is when the examiner looks at his or her motives as to why he is approaching God. The person has to look inside himself and examine his heart to see if his worship is about himself or about God.

Expectation is the aspect of worship that when people come to worship God, they expect Him to show up in an atmospheric way. It is the belief that if you come to worship, God will meet with you.

Appropriation is putting into action the human activity part of worship. Worship is about offering what is appropriate; a person cannot worship or meet with God without putting himself or herself out there. They have to act.

Meditation is worshipping God reverently. While some choose to sing aloud and make more demonstrative movements, meditation is just quietly reverencing the Lord. During the meditation element of worship, a person just reflects on the things of God and the character and nature of God.

Dr. Jason Whitehurst

Consummation is the conclusion to the worship experience. The conclusion is not just a benediction prayer, but it is a dedicated and changed life as a result of the time of worship. You cannot enter into the presence of God and go away unchanged.

Transformation is that worship must do more than lead to dedication. It must lead to transformation. Worship is transformative because during worship you realize what you can't do, and when you realize what you can't do, you realize how great God is.

There is music that points people to God and music that does not point people to God. Music that does point people to God is seen in 2 Chronicles 5:11–14, which says,

> And when the priests came out of the Holy Place (for all the priests who were present had consecrated themselves, without regard to their divisions, and all the Levitical singers, Asaph, Heman, and Jeduthun, their sons and kinsmen, arrayed in fine linen, with cymbals, harps, and lyres, stood east of the altar with 120 priests who were trumpeters; and it was the duty of the trumpeters and singers to make themselves heard in unison in praise and thanksgiving to the LORD), AND WHEN THE SONG WAS RAISED, WITH TRUMPETS AND CYMBALS AND OTHER MUSICAL INSTRUMENTS, IN PRAISE TO THE LORD, "FOR HE IS GOOD, FOR HIS STEADFAST LOVE ENDURES FOREVER, "THE HOUSE, THE HOUSE OF THE LORD, WAS FILLED WITH A CLOUD, so that the priests could not stand to minister because of the cloud, for the glory of the LORD FILLED THE HOUSE OF GOD.

Another reason creating a worship environment that is effective and ministers to ADD congregants is that worship has been linked

May I Have Your Attention Please?

with church growth primarily because worship services are becoming primarily the entry point for people into the church.[57] Every pastor or minister wants to be a part of a church that is growing and thriving; that is common sense. It is therefore vital that the worship service really be a focal point of pastors and ministers, recognizing church growth is being seen in a great way through the worship service, and that it is the "front door" for people trying the church out.

Growing churches have enthusiastic and celebrative worship services. In creating the atmosphere for worship, the five elements that are important in creating the right worship environment, according to Thom Rainer, are celebrative, friendly, expectant, relaxed, and positive.[58] These five elements are great and should be sought after. But what also must be factored in or considered is the condition of a person's heart when he enters a worship service. If he has a bad attitude or a lack of gratitude, the worship service can be designed to include all five elements that Rainer lists, and it will not matter. It is the same way that someone can go to a celebratory party, such as a birthday party or a retirement party, and by having the wrong attitude will not have an enjoyable moment, no matter how great the party is. The same holds true when it comes to worship services.

When the two reasons are combined that worship is biblical and integral part of the life of the believer, and that the churches that are growing are the ones that have lively, celebrative, energetic worship services, the significance of ensuring the worship service of a church is effective in engaging and ministering to ADD or ADHD congregants is evident. If people with ADD visit a church and the worship service is boring and does not promote biblical worship as Jesus outlined, he or she will not continue to attend that church.

The Planning of the Environment

There is a saying, "If you fail to plan, you plan to fail." If there is no effort on the part of the pastor or minister or church council to plan for an effective worship environment for ADD or ADHD congregants, there will be no effective worship environment. It has to be intentional; it usually will not occur by accident. The leaders of the church must be onboard, on the same page, and see a vision where there is a worship atmosphere and environment that is consistent each Sunday that meets the needs and overcomes the obstacles facing ADD congregants.

A church should be on the move. It should be trying to become what God wants it to become. In this sense, it is on a trip. There needs to be a plan for this trip. There should be questions asked, such as why, who, when, and at what expense, and these questions should be answered as a part of the church's plan. This plan is more than just a trip plan; it is a plan for ministry. This is often referred to as the church's program.[59]

A church program is what you do as an expression of your awareness and commitment to the church's purpose and objectives. It should be planned in relation to the needs of the people, both in and out of the fellowship. It is what a church does to be obedient to Christ in trying to live His way and to be faithful in working with Him to bring people to God.

The planning stage is not always easy, it is not always agreed upon, and there is not always unity among the members of a council or a committee as to what the plan should be. There are disagreements over objectives. Any time changed is involved, it is not always palatable to the entire church body.

If a church is going to effectively create the environment needed by ADD congregants to engage in the spiritual act of worship, proper planning must take place. The pastor or minister has to cast the vision, and the church council and church body need to trust that God has placed the vision in the pastor's heart, and by faith, act on that plan. Scripture states in Hebrews 11:6a, "Without faith, it is impossible to please Him" (ESV).

There is an idea I suggest for churches that do not already serve coffee or espresso prior to their Sunday morning worship service. I propose that churches offer espresso, cappuccino, or coffee an hour before the Sunday morning worship service. In my experience, I've found that offering this helps those with ADD to receive a more meaningful time of worship. It also provides a time of fellowship for all the congregants before services.

There will always be boundaries and barriers to cross and overcome any time planning takes place, as has been noted. Human beings are creatures of habit and get set in their ways, so when a new idea, concept, or way of doing things appears, many people are reluctant to embrace the plan. Churches get so comfortable with

Dr. Jason Whitehurst

what they do that they are hesitant to make any changes, to do anything differently, to make any ripples or go against the grain, or try anything new. Someone once asked me, "If you could change one thing about your church or ministry that has never been done, but if it was done would totally change the dynamic of the church forever, what would that one thing be?" My answer was, "I'd create an environment that ministers to ADD congregants. It would change the dynamics of the church."

The Music of the Environment

In an environment that effectively reaches and ministers to ADD and ADHD congregants in a worship service, the music needs to be different. The music needs to be more contemporary and with a full array of instruments, not just an organ or a single piano. If your church does not have a variety of instruments, you may be interested in getting the DVDs that are available.

Those with ADD or ADHD are not going to be able to stay focused on boring, monotone music during the worship service. Going back to the symptoms of ADD or ADHD, the major categories include inattentiveness and hyperactivity. Therefore, the music must address these needs if it is going to be effective.

Church music has been a sticking point for many church members for years, going back in church history to when some of the hymns were considered contemporary or too "edgy." Christians disagree about music styles in the church as much as any other issue in the body of Christ.[60] Each member has

May I Have Your Attention Please?

his or her own personal tastes and preferences. The question that has to be answered is this: what is captivating and upbeat enough to keep the attention of those with ADD and offset any hyperactivity with those who suffer from that symptom yet is still biblical worship music?

The apostle Paul said in Ephesians 5:19, "addressing one another in psalms and hymns and spiritual songs, singing and making melody to the Lord with your heart" (ESV). These are the three types of songs addressed in the Bible. Singing psalms is singing the words of Scripture. Singing hymns is singing worship music to God. Singing spiritual songs is singing music with lyrics that express our testimony.[61]

The first aspect of church music is the singing of psalms. The book of Psalms has been described as the hymnbook of the Old Testament. A number of other portions of the Old and New Testaments may have been written as psalms celebrating the greatness of God.

Throughout church history, Scripture has been sung in different ways, from Gregorian chants in the Middle Ages to singing psalms from the Psalter during the Reformation. Today, psalms are sung with electric guitars and drums and other instruments.

The second aspect of church music is hymns. Our idea of hymns is not what Paul was talking about when he wrote his letter to the Ephesians. A simple definition of a hymn is a song about or to God. Hymns are designed to cause Christians to think and meditate on the character and nature of God.

The third aspect of church music is spiritual songs. These songs are celebratory of the relationship the believer has with God. These songs relate to the Christian living and delve into the unbelievably rich encounters a believer has with God. Spiritual songs are more prevalent in contemporary type of churches.

With each different style of song, there are different styles of music. These songs can be sung in a rock and roll style, a country-western style, an acoustical style, and many more. More than the type of song or style, the important thing is that the music that is played and sung is not just captivating or dynamic or contemporary but that it honors God.

In their book, *Perimeters of Light: Biblical Boundaries for the Emerging Church*, Elmer Towns and Ed Stetzer discuss seven test questions to determine whether the music we sing is Christ honoring. They are

1. *The Message Test* – Does the song come from the Word of God? Is the message of the God spiritually edifying and uplifting?

2. *The Purpose Test* – What is the emotion that is trying to be elicited from the song? What does the leader want the audience to feel as they sing?

3. *The Association Test* – Does the song identify with things, actions, or people that are not Christian?

4. *The Memory Test* – Does the song bring back things from the past that you have left?

5. *The Proper Emotions Test* – Does the song stir our emotions in a negative way and cause negative or lustful feelings?

6. *The Understanding Test* – Will the listeners have a hard time understanding the words or the message or finding the melody?

7. *The Music Test* – Is there a song within the song?[62]

Every church must assess if the music they sing each Sunday would pass these seven tests. If not, then the music needs to be addressed. If it does not glorify God and bring about spiritual edification in the believer, it is not worship music.

The music that may minister to ADD or ADHD congregants may vary from church to church and from city to city. What works in Seattle, Washington, may not work in Houston, Texas. What works in Boston, Massachusetts, may not work in San Diego, California. It is not because those with ADD or ADHD in those areas have different forms of the disease; it is that there is no one style that will address the situation at every church. What is important is not the style but finding the right style that ministers to the ADD congregants in your area, and that honors God first and foremost.

Dr. Jason Whitehurst

The Multisensory Environment

Along with the music, which stirs the emotions of men and women and touches the senses, there are other tools and resources that can be used in a worship service to engage multiple senses at one time to create an environment that is effective for ADD people. When what is going on in the environment engages more than just one sense, it helps to offset some of the tendencies and symptoms of ADD. These resources all make sense and are practical in light of the symptoms of the disease.

The first such resource is PowerPoint or visual media. Many churches are using PowerPoint for the sermons or messages and also for the music. If someone with ADD is singing, while reading the words on the screen, they are being engaged on multiple levels. They have to process several senses at once.

Also, using video clips is a great tool to grab the attention of those with ADD or ADHD. Churches are using the technology available more and more. Short video clips can be dynamic in getting a poignant message or even an announcement across, and it hits the audience on several sensory levels.

Many churches are now using theatrical or stage lighting to set the environment or atmosphere. Depending on the mood they want to set, they will have certain colors showing. These lights, just like in a production or play, can be used to great effect in a worship service. For example, if an upbeat song is being sung, there would be plenty of bright colors like yellows and other warm colors. If the mood or atmosphere that is desired is more subdued or somber, blues or

May I Have Your Attention Please?

cool colors are used to set that environment. Many churches are already being built this way. It used to be that the church was filled with lots of light—natural and electric—and stained-glass windows. Contemporary music and drama require a purposefully lit stage in order to highlight performers. Traditional church design, with its cascade of natural sunlight, works against controlled lighting's effectiveness.[63]

Some churches are even going to laser light shows. For churches that are creating increasingly contemporary worship services or hosting Christian musicians, the same laser light effects used in television commercials and music videos can enhance the visual impact of worship services and Christian music artist concerts.

For example, a water screen is used with a laser light show as a moving and shimmering projection screen. Lasers can project an intense image that appears on the water screen. As the water pours from an upper distribution pipe and falls into a shallow trough, the lasers project computer-driven images or movies onto the falling water droplets like a traditional movie projector onto a hanging white projection screen. For church presentation, a water screen can be used to display moving spiritual images or scenic backdrops for musicians' performances.[64]

Clearly, this is an extravagant example, and not many churches can afford to have these kinds of visual tools. There are lighting fixtures for churches of every size and budget. They may not be Disney-quality laser lights, but canned lights and gels can be

Dr. Jason Whitehurst

purchased rather inexpensively if a church desires to use lighting to create the environment.

There are many churches that use multisensory tools. One such church is Bridge International Church in Rotterdam. The pastor of the church said, "It's almost like going into a nightclub and seeing a secular Christian band perform," said James Bookhout of the band of musicians that rock the house during praise and worship. "It enhances the worship experience."[65]

Some Christians would be turned off by a church that closely resembles a club. Many pastors and church leaders would probably like to stay away from having their sanctuary look like the hottest nightclub in the city. The example of Bridge International Church is an extreme example. Each church has to decide what it feels comfortable with when it comes to using multisensory tools. Every church is different, and what I would suggest is to use as many tools as the church is comfortable with, but no more than that because then the opposite effect of what you are trying to achieve occurs. The purpose of multisensory tools is to have more engagement and more focus, not for church members to be distracted during the worship service.

Concerning a multisensory atmosphere and environment, Mark Driscoll, pastor of Mars Hill in Seattle, Washington, said, "Everything in the service needs to preach—architecture, lighting, songs, prayers, fellowship, the smell—it all preaches. All five senses must be engaged to experience God."[66] Something stands out about what Driscoll states about the senses. I find it very

May I Have Your Attention Please?

interesting that Driscoll includes the sense of smell and makes the assertion that the way a sanctuary or auditorium smells impacts the preaching aspect of the service. I believe what Driscoll is saying that the way your building smells can trigger a conscious or subconscious response. A foul smell can distract or hinder because a person is more focused on the smell than the service. On the flip side, a pleasant or fresh smell can trigger a desired positive response.

I will give you an example. Have you ever been to an old, rundown movie theater that reeked of mold and mildew and just smelled plan nasty? The odor was everywhere in the theater. How much did you enjoy that movie? Were you hindered from having the best possible experience and getting all that you could out of the movie because of the odor? Conversely, have you been to a movie theater where the place was well kept and the smell of the building was fresh and clean? Did you get more out of the movie because you felt more comfortable and not disturbed by a foul smell? Which theater are you likely to go back to? There is a connection between our sense of smell and how it affects us in a given environment. The same is true in churches.

Dan Kimball adds this on the sense of smell in churches: "How ironic that returning to a raw and ancient form of worship is now seen as new and even cutting edge. We are simply going back to a vintage form of worship which has been around for as long as the church has been in existence."[67] Kimball seems to be putting a different slant than Driscoll.

Dr. Jason Whitehurst

Kimball is referring to a movement in America today that is extremely popular among college students and young adults. The movement is based on how the early church met in caves. It is based on how there are churches in China and other parts of the world that meet in remote locations that have a smell to them which is raw and unique. If you have ever gone into a mine, you know the kind of smell Kimball is referring to. The point he is making is the way that location smells triggers a response and stimulates the senses. There is a heightened sense of your surroundings, which brings increased focus. Kimball's point is that it is interesting that this form of meeting environment is perceived as cutting edge but that it is catching on in many places. Actually, churches who are meeting in settings like this that are having services that for six or seven hours. And people stay and are engaged. The conclusion is that the sense of smell is powerful when it comes to multisensory atmospheres.

What does all this mean for those with ADD and ADHD? It means that churches are adapting to make their worship services more "ADD-friendly." It may not be a conscious effort in every case to specifically reach those with ADD or ADHD, but the end result is the same; many churches across America that are using multisensory technology and concepts are seeing tremendous growth.

Churches with a multisensory atmosphere will also limit distractions. They keep things moving. There is always something going on to keep the attention of the audience member. In churches that are traditional in the sense that they are not multisensory, just one little thing can be a distraction, such as a cough or a sneeze or someone getting up to go out of the sanctuary or auditorium. In a multisensory environment, because it is more relaxed, people do not pick up on these things as much, so they are not as likely to get distracted by them.

I'm not saying every pastor or church leader should go out and buy a laser light kit or theatrical lighting. Not every church can do that with its budget, nor should it try without bathing it in prayer. I'm just saying that a pastor or church leader has to do something to create an environment that grabs and keeps the attention of those with ADD or ADHD, so that they are being ministered to in the worship service.

What Churches Can Learn from the School Environment

The school system is seeking to include students with ADD or ADHD and make them feel a part of what is going on in the classroom. They are taking great lengths so that these students do not feel ostracized or like they do not belong. The school system came up with strategies based on research and knowledge about the disease. They are all based upon the principle that by creating a better fit between the school environment and the student, we are creating opportunities for him or her to succeed. Students with ADD/ADHD often experience difficulties in mainstream classrooms and schools because the emphasis on meeting common needs means that their specific needs are not addressed.[68] If there is no emphasis on meeting their needs and engaging the students with methods based on the latest research, students with ADD or ADHD will struggle to learn, and it will reflect poorly on their grades.

There are several things that the school systems have found in dealing with students with ADD or ADHD that should be implemented in the church. Pastors and ministers can learn from the successes the schools have had.

The first example is the attitude of teachers toward students with ADD or ADHD. Recent research by Ghanizadeh, Bahredar, and Moeini demonstrated that more tolerant and positive attitudes toward students with ADHD are associated with levels of knowledge of ADHD among teachers. This suggests that training to increase teachers' knowledge of ADHD may need to be a priority if subsequent shifts in attitudes and practice are to occur.[69]

Research shows that the more teachers knew about ADD and ADHD, the better they understood and related to the students. Transposing that principle to the church world, the more that pastors and ministers know about ADD, the more they can relate and understand their ADD congregants.

The school system also discussed minimizing distractions. Students with AD/HD have a lower threshold for distraction than other students. As such, it is important to create a classroom environment that accommodates this difference whenever possible.

May I Have Your Attention Please?

For example, the student may need to be given preferential seating in a place that is as free from distraction as possible, for instance, away from doors and windows, and in an area of the classroom with a direct line of sight to the teacher.[70]

If pastors could eliminate more distractions, they would be so much more effective in creating an environment for ADD congregants as the schools are creating for the students. Things like making sure cell phones are turned off, not allowing any babies into the sanctuary unless they are newborns, having ushers ready to handle any distractions, and not having windows in the sanctuary for people to look out and get distracted.

A great way to get the message across to turn off cell phones or take babies to the nursery is to having scrolling announcements prior to the service on the screens. My church does this. If you do not have a projector and screens in your church, you can put a section in the bulletin with the same requests or have designated greeters who will kindly address someone who they see has a cell phone on or is trying to bring a baby into the sanctuary.

Also in my church, we have an older sanctuary with lots of windows, so we have the ability to pull down blinds to keep the congregation from looking outside into the parking lot and becoming distracted.

Another finding was that predictability and establishing a routine was very successful with students. Students with ADHD will benefit

Dr. Jason Whitehurst

from being provided with a clear structure to each day, lesson, and task. When introducing lessons, it is useful to

- review the previous lesson (remind them of what the key topics and concepts were and explain how they link to the current lesson);

- provide an advance outline/schedule (talk students through the order of the various activities planned for the current lesson);

- set learning expectations (make clear what and how they will learn);

- set behavioral expectations (explain what is and is not acceptable, and how and when this could change during the lesson—for example, that talking with other students is acceptable during a group activity but not during a test);

- state needed materials and resources (explain what students will need to complete the various activities and where they can find these materials); and

- simplify instructions and choices (ensure that these are communicated in a clear, uncomplicated manner).[71]

The next chapter will deal with this concept more, on communicating in a better way to those with ADD or ADHD, but the principle is clear that those with ADD learn better

May I Have Your Attention Please?

and respond better when they are in an environment that is repetitive and there is a routine so they know what to expect. This does not mean pastors and ministers should make church services as boring and routine as possible. The concept is of the ADD congregants having some familiarity with what is going. For instance, if the pastor is doing a series of sermons, use the opening part to refresh what has been gone over in previous weeks and then go from there.

These are just some of the things the school system has found out through research on how to make the classroom a better learning environment, for teachers to be more effective in teaching their students. Pastors and ministers can glean a lot of valuable concepts through what is being learned and how effective these teachers are now being based on the knowledge they have been empowered with.

In conclusion, creating the right environment for ADD or ADHD congregants has to be intentional. The principles and concepts laid out in this chapter will aid a pastor, minister, or church leader in creating such an environment that those who suffer from the disease will be engaged in the worship service and as a result will be effectively ministered to.

To reiterate, it is important that a conducive environment be created for ADD congregants, because as human beings, the sole purpose God created man was for fellowship and worship. If a church wants to be the place where people can come and experience and be engaged in corporate worship as a part of the creation design in a group setting, there must be things in place for the worship service that assist in engaging those with ADD or ADHD. It is biblical that they worship God as Christians; therefore, there needs to be a setting in place that enables them to worship and not distract or detract. With proper planning, this kind of environment can be created. God will be glorified, and the church will be edified.

Endnotes:

1. Elmer L. Towns and Ed Stetzer, Perimeters of Light: Biblical Boundaries for the Emerging Church (Chicago: Moody Publishers, 2004), 75.
2. Ibid.
3. Ibid., 85.
4. Thom S. Rainer, The Book of Church Growth: History, Theology, and Principles (Nashville, TN: Broadman Press, 1993), 225.
5. Ibid., 228.
6. Charles A. Tidwell, Church Administration: Effective Leadership for Ministry (Nashville, TN: Broadman Press, 1985), 91.
7. Towns and Stetzer, Perimeters of Light, 95.
8. Towns and Stetzer, Perimeters of Light, 97.
9. Ibid., 103.
10. Kent Morris, "Stage Lighting for Modern Worship ChurchBuyersGuide.com." Christianity Today: A Magazine of Evangelical Conviction. http://www.christianitytoday.com/cbg/2005/sepoct/2.33.html (accessed April 9, 2012).
11. Ibid.
12. Paul Nelson, "Church Aims to Make Service Comfortable: Bridge Christian Provides Short Sermons, Theatrical Worship and Relaxing Atmosphere." Times Union (Albany, NY) (February 21, 2007): Newspaper Source Plus, EBSCOhost (accessed April 9, 2012).

13. "The National Reevaluation Forum: The Story of the Gathering," Youth Leader Networks - NEXT Special Edition, 1999, pp. 3–8, citing Mark Driscoll, "Themes of the Emerging Church."
14. Dan Kimball, The Emerging Church: Vintage Christianity for New Generations (Grand Rapids, MI: Zondervan, 2003), 169.
15. Neil Humphrey, "Including Students with Attention-Deficit/Hyperactivity Disorder in Mainstream Schools." British Journal of Special Education 36, no. 1 (March 2009): 19–25. Academic Search Complete, EBSCOhost (accessed April 2, 2012).
16. Ibid.
17. Ibid.
18. Ibid., 22.

Chapter 3

Preaching Effectively to Those with ADD and ADHD

A vital part of a worship service each week is the sermon or message. The sermon is just as important as the music portion of the worship service; it is an integral part of the worship experience for church members. The problem is that just hearing the word *sermon* has a negative connotation with some church members. They automatically think of this as the boring part of the service where the pastor or minister stands in front of them, never leaving the pulpit, and proceeds for thirty to forty-five minutes to wax eloquent with three points and a poem. But that is not how sermons should be, and if they are to minister to ADD sufferers, they cannot be boring, dull, monotonous messages that are being preached or taught each Sunday.

There is a biblical basis for the topic of effectively communicating a message or sermon to those who have short attention spans or are inattentive or overly hyper. Jesus set the example in His ministry

Dr. Jason Whitehurst

by preaching those who had diseases or issues. Jesus communicated a message or a sermon by sharing a parable.

Jesus felt it was important during His ministry to speak in parables, because when He spoke in parables, everyone could understand. Jesus took profound truth and used a simple, short story to convey a deep principle. Jesus showed the importance of getting the message across, not trying to preach home-run, exegetical sermons but communicating in an effective way so that people got the message. Everyone could understand parables.

To avoid the stigma of the negative connotation associated with sermons, sermons are now being called different things by Andy Stanley and other preachers and teachers across America. *Sermons, talks, teachings,* and *messages* can be used interchangeably. Also, there is no distinction among preaching, teaching, or general communicating. It goes without saying that not every pastor or minister would agree with Stanley's assessment, but these words are being used interchangeably by prominent pastors and communicators across the country, such as Louie Giglio, Mark Driscoll, and Reggie Joyner.

The purpose of this chapter is to examine how a pastor, preacher, teacher, communicator, or church leader, can effectively communicate to those in the congregation with ADD or ADHD. I will discuss different aspects and facets of preaching, as well as different styles of preaching that can be effective in those with ADD if pastors and preachers will utilize the styles as they are meant to be used.

May I Have Your Attention Please?

Effective preaching must be engaging. By now, it has been established what ADD and ADHD are and what the symptoms of ADD and ADHD are. If a sermon or message or talk is to be effective, it has to engage the listener who suffers from the disease, who is inattentive, daydreaming, or hyperactive. Based on the knowledge of ADD and ADHD that we know, the data would suggest that it is easier to keep those with ADD or ADHD engaged during the singing part of the worship service than the preaching part of the worship service. During the preaching or communicating time, the ADD sufferer has to sit in a chair or a pew and try to focus and also not be a distraction to those around him or her. The person must be engaged by the message or talk.

Jeff Foxworthy, a very popular comedian who has made a living off engaging people with humor through standup comedy, said, "To communicate effectively, you have to connect." He adds that a communicator needs to leverage his connection as a communicator to teach people the truth of God's love, to make it personal for the listener, and to show him how to live the life he was meant to live.

The goal of every pastor or teacher is to communicate the Word of God in a way that the listener receives it, processes it, and digests it. At least that should be the goal, based on 2 Timothy 4:2, which says, "Preach the word; be ready in season and out of season; reprove, rebuke, and exhort, with complete patience and teaching" (ESV). Paul was not telling young Timothy to preach because he enjoyed hearing the sound of his own voice, or to preach God's Word because it was his job, but the command Paul gives is speaking of preaching the Word in order that the listener might be edified and encouraged. This includes those who live with ADD or ADHD on a daily basis. They need to have the Bible preached or taught to them so that they may grow spiritually. Therefore, the message or sermon or talk must connect so that the ADD congregant can receive it, process it, and digest it.

Hopefully by the end of this chapter, there will concepts and ideas discussed and examined that will show pastors, teachers, or communicators how to effectively address those in their fellowship that have ADD. It is important to note that some of the things presented in this chapter will not be universally recognized as valid or a good way to go about preaching or communicating. The goal of the author is not to start a controversy but to present methods of preaching, teaching, and communicating that can be effective in reaching the goal of the pastor, teacher, or communicator, which is to get the sermon or message across. On some things presented, the pastor or minister reading this project may have to agree to disagree. But the pastor or minister should consider the material presented not in the light of his or her own personal preference or tastes but in light of what is effective in ministering to those with ADD.

The Effectiveness of Preaching Delivery

A pastor, preacher, or communicator must be aware of his own delivery. It is possible that the way that a pastor or communicator has been delivering messages is defective. Speech specialists agree

May I Have Your Attention Please?

that one's speech delivery needs corrective treatment if it falls under one of three conditions: if the delivery calls attention to itself, if the delivery interferes with effective communication, or if the delivery creates self-consciousness or causes anxiety.[72]

There is always the possibility that the delivery is defective and not effective but that it could be more effective if the pastor or communicator was aware of how ineffective he is. His own judgment of himself may be unreliable, and therefore he needs more criteria to judge his delivery. The following questions are submitted to assess the effectiveness of one's delivery:

1. Do you ever have trouble with your throat after speaking? Are you hoarse at such times? Does your throat feel strained or tired?

2. What is the quality of the attention given you by your congregation? Do they listen avidly?

3. Do you know your own speech machine, as a mechanic knows his automobile?

4. Do you actually know the many different elements that enter into effective vocal expression? Are you making the best use of them?

5. Have you ever had your speaking voice analyzed?

6. Did you ever think about the emotional message which people get from you? What do you feel about yourself?

7. What do you do with your body when speaking?

8. Have you ever really settled that difficult question about the use of notes or manuscript?[73]

These questions all should be considered, and sober and truthful answers should be given. Any pastor or communicator should want to have an effective delivery, and if it is not being effective and the pastor or communicator recognizes that based on the listed questions, then steps should be taken to work on the delivery of the message.

There are also voice variables, which are aspects of delivery. Many people never consider these voice variables and how important they are. The voice variables are pitch, range, intonation, and inflection.[74]

Pitch refers to the sound the vocal chords make when they are closed and air passes through them. Pitch is often determined by a thought or feeling. There is an optimal pitch that is aesthetically pleasing.

Range is the distance between the lowest pitch and highest pitch a person has. A pastor or communicator who has a wide range and uses it frequently will generally be more interesting.

Intonation is a speaker's use of range within a sentence. It means that a speaker's speech is not haphazard but makes a tune, or a melody.

Inflection is a glide within one syllable of a word in which a person expresses sarcasm, conviction, doubt, or any other expression of attitude. Inflections are important to a speaker's message because they carry the real meaning and feeling behind what the speaker is saying. Inflection signifies the emotion intended for the audience to receive.

Mastering the vocal delivery of a message or talk will enhance the effectiveness that the message has on the audience. It is common sense to know and understand that a pastor or communicator who is monotone is not as likely to capture the attention of the audience as a pastor or communicator who has vocal variety. By using vocal variety, changing the loudness or softness at key moments of the message, and using different inflections that convey various emotions, a communicator can grab the attention of the ADD congregant and keep it. When a pastor understands the science behind vocal variables, he will be much more effective overall, not just with ADD or ADHD congregants.

Everyone has heard a person speak, and afterward, whether it was a speech or a sermon or a monologue in a play, the message stuck because the speaker's vocal delivery was diverse. The aim here is to shed light so that pastors and communicators will examine their delivery in light of this knowledge, and if they are not being effective, that they will have a sober assessment and become effective in their delivery. It will only help their cause in preaching or teaching to people with ADD.

The Effectiveness of Expository Preaching

Expository preaching is a style of preaching that can be effective in ministering to those with ADD or ADHD. But not everyone agrees that expository preaching, or any preaching for that matter, is an urgent need of the church. There are those that believe there are other ministries and methods that are better and more in tune with the times. However, the writers of the New Testament understood the importance of preaching.

Preaching stands as the event through which God works.[75] Peter said in 1 Peter 1:23, "Since you have been born again, not of perishable seed but of imperishable, through the living and abiding word of God" (ESV). Peter went on to say in 1 Peter 1:25, "And this word is the good news that was preached to you" (ESV). The people were redeemed because the "word" had been preached to them. Preaching is important. It should not be relegated to a thing of the past or minimized by some churches but embraced, because it is preaching or communicating the good news of the gospel that changes lives.

With that in mind, expository preaching is needed. Expository preaching is defined as the communication of a biblical concept, derived from and transmitted through a historical, grammatical, and literary study of a passage in its context, which the Holy Spirit first applies to the personality and experience of the preacher, then through the preacher, applies to the hearers.[76]

Basically, expository preaching is taking a verse or passage and doing a total and complete analysis of it, such as the historical context, the grammatical context, the type of literary form, and then using all of that data to put together the message. It is the work of the Holy Spirit to first "preach" it to the preacher so that he owns it, so that he can go deliver the sermon with passion and fervor because he feels it. The idea is you cannot powerfully preach what you do not feel, and the message is powerful because it is well conceived and formulated based on a thorough analysis of the text.

Expository Preaching Is Biblically Accurate

Expository preaching is more of a philosophy than a method. Preachers must ask themselves whether they bend their thoughts to the Scriptures or use the Scriptures to support their thoughts. They should consider whether they try to make the text say something it does not in order to support their beliefs or whether they allow the text to tell them what they should believe. Expository preaching says that the preacher does not speak to the text, but the text is to speak to the preacher. Preachers have a tendency to cherry-pick verses to make a point. But the text cannot mean something now that it did not mean to the writer when he wrote it.

Expository Preaching Is Conceptual

Expository preaching emphasizes the communication of a concept. It does not emphasize just what a word means, but it underscores a concept that a given text or group of words dictates to the pastor or communicator.[77] The thrust of this style of preaching is to let the text speak for itself and for the communicator or pastor to simply preach the concept that is being presented as is, without putting his own personal spin on it. Unfortunately, many preachers and communicators do not practice this. They claim to be expository preachers or communicators, yet they use verses as launching pads for their own personal opinions.[78]

Anyone who has been in church long enough has come across a preacher who totally mishandles a passage of Scripture to put a spin on it to get his personal opinion across. What these preachers are really saying when they do that is that their personal belief is more important than the message the text is actually conveying. Of course, they would not say that audibly, but their actions communicate it loudly and clearly. These are "one-string banjo" preachers: they have a banjo with one string and they play that one string every week. No matter what the text is, they find a way to tie it in with their "one string."

An example I have seen of this is prosperity theology preaching. Not all prosperity theology preachers, but most, have that "one string," and they play it every week. Doesn't matter what the text is. They will somehow find a way to twist it to say, "God wants you to be wealthy." I am not kidding or making this up. I have been to churches and every message was the same thing. It didn't matter if it was Easter, Mother's Day, or Christmas, "God wants you to be rich" was the message. That is a gross mishandling of the Word of God, and it promotes an erroneous view of God. Do I believe God blesses His people financially? Absolutely. Do I believe there are verses that discuss the blessings and favor of God? For sure. Should a preacher take John 3:16 or any other text and spin it to promote prosperity theology where it does not apply? Definitely not.

Expository Preaching Is Applicable

One reason expository preaching can be effective to those with ADD or ADHD is that it is applicable. Application gives expository preaching purpose.[79] Expository sermons without effective applications are usually dull. An example of an application point is if a communicator was giving a sermon or talk on the life of Gideon. One of the points of application is that God does not see you as you see yourself. Gideon saw himself as a coward, but God saw him as a mighty man. Another application in the story of Gideon is that God uses the most unlikely people to great things for His glory and purpose. No one would've chosen Gideon. He was from the least of the tribes of Israel, the least in his family, and a coward. But God uses people the world wouldn't pick to do great things by His power.

With ADD and ADHD in mind, this style of preaching would make sense in how it could be effective in capturing the minds and attention of those who suffer from the disease. Sermons, messages, or talks that utilize good applications are generally effective in the author's experience. They are more real and genuine than just a verse-by-verse exegesis of the text. It is great to know what the original language means or what the author was going through

Dr. Jason Whitehurst

when he wrote the book in the Bible, but how does it apply to the listener? That is really what people want to know, not just knowledge for knowledge sake but how what is being preached, taught, or communicated applies to their lives.

Expository Preaching Is Culturally Relevant

Another reason that expository preaching can be effective is that it says forget about speaking to the ages and speak to the people today. A congregation does not gather to convict Judas, Peter, or Solomon but to judge themselves. Expository preachers say they must know the people as well as the message.[80] An expository message should be a bullet, not a buckshot. Ideally, each sermon is the explanation, interpretation, or application of a single dominant idea supported by other ideas. It should relate biblical truths to the people of today.

Use personal stories as illustrations. Write things down as they happen in your life or in the lives of people you know, and use them as sermon illustrations. Pastors can also go to many places online to get contemporary, culturally relevant video clips and illustrations. I recommend that pastors or communicators read pop culture magazines or watch some of the more popular TV shows. There are plenty of culturally relevant applications to be drawn from these resources.

May I Have Your Attention Please?

Expository Preaching Is Meant to Stick

Years ago, Calvin Coolidge returned home from church one Sunday and was asked by his wife what the minister had talked about. Coolidge replied, "Sin." When his wife pressed him as to what the preacher said about sin, Coolidge responded, "I think he was against it." The truth is many people in the pew leave church and do not remember the sermon, just as Calvin Coolidge didn't.

Those who hear expository preaching should be able to answer the question of what they heard that day. They should be able to recall the message or talk. Expository preaching that is truly expository will not leave the listener in a mental fog about what they listened to. The danger is that with that mental fog would come spiritual peril.

This is why expository preaching is a viable and valuable style of preaching that will be effective in ministering to those with ADD. It is designed, it its truest form, to leave the hearer of the message or talk with a lasting impression. It is meant to engage the listener with applications and relation to current culture so that the congregant remembers the message and as a result gleans something from it and grows from it. Expository preaching in its truest form is effective in ministering to those with ADD or ADHD.

I was preaching to the Virginia High School State Champion track team from Western Branch High School in Chesapeake, Virginia, and I used an illustration that made the message stick. I know that it stuck because months later, these students remembered what I said on a Sunday morning and what my point was.

Dr. Jason Whitehurst

The illustration was of the long jump exhibit in Atlanta, where the Olympics were held. They had it measured out how long the longest jump in track and field history was, which was twenty-seven feet and a few inches. I got a tape measure and stood at the front of the sanctuary and had one of the track team members come up and assist me. I prefaced the illustration with the backstory of how I was going to show them the farthest that a man had ever jumped, which at the time was Carl Lewis.

I played it up and took my time with the illustration. I stretched the measuring tape out a good distance, paused, and said, "No, that's not it." I did this a few times, building anticipation and tension with the audience. Finally, I stretched the tape measure out the full twenty-seven feet and however many inches. It covered nearly the entire width of the sanctuary. I asked the track team and the rest of the church that day if anyone besides Carl Lewis could make that jump. Of course the answer was no; it was an impossible distance. No one could ever successfully jump that far in one single leap.

And then I hit them with it. I said, "Just like it is impossible for anyone to jump this great distance, this great divide, it is impossible for you to get to God on your own, in your human ability. You can't do it. The distance is too great. The only way you can reach God is through what Jesus did on the cross. He made the jump, and He is the only person in the history of the world who could bridge the great distance between God and man spiritually." Those guys and girls still remember the message of the cross and the love of God because of that illustration.

Pastors, think about your ADD and ADHD congregants, and if you can make it stick with them, it will stick with everyone else as well.

The Effectiveness of Multisensory Preaching

Multisensory preaching is not groundbreaking to some pastors. But to those church leaders who have been behind the eight ball and are looking for fresh and engaging ways to speak to their congregants without losing them because of the changes being made, this concept may be mind-blowing.

Multisensory preaching is preaching or communicating that touches on more than just one sense. Unlike conventional preaching, which stimulates only the sense of hearing, multisensory communication stimulates multiple senses: hearing, seeing, touching, and sometimes even smell and taste.[81] Multisensory preaching or communication brings more of the whole person into the teaching process.

The Need for Multisensory Preaching

Based on what is known about ADD and ADHD, multisensory preaching is a great style to use because it stimulates the brain and engages the senses so that a person who has trouble paying attention or sitting still is locked when his or her senses are activated.

Author Rick Blackwood, pastor of Christ Fellowship Church writes,

> I'll never forget the first color television my dad purchased. Finally, we were going to

see television programs in living color. To help us receive broadcast signals, Dad purchased a high-powered, multiangle antenna. It rotated in a complete 360-degree circle, which gave it the capacity to receive multiple channels. At that time, there were basically three networks on the air: ABC, NBC, and CBS. In other words, Hollywood had the capacity to communicate through three networks, and our multiangle antenna gave us the capacity to receive all three. Unfortunately, even with this high-powered antenna, we received only one channel clearly — NBC. Why only one channel? The answer was simple: ABC did not broadcast any signal to Rock Hill, South Carolina, and CBS did not broadcast a clear signal.

On the receiving end, our TV was wired to receive all three channels: ABC, NBC, and CBS. But only one channel communicated to our television — NBC. The communication breakdown was not on the receiving end. It was on the communicating end. This is the picture of much modern-day preaching. The breakdown in communication is often on the teacher's end. As biblical teachers, we have three sensory channels by which to communicate information — verbal, visual, and interactive. Corresponding to that three-dimensional communication, the people in our congregation have a three-channel neurological antenna by which to receive that information. They can hear the verbal communication, they can see the visuals, and they can touch the interactive elements. But in most churches, the information is broadcast in one channel only — verbal. At Christ Fellowship Church, we try to communicate from all three channels (verbal, visual, and interactive) to the corresponding senses of reception (hearing, seeing, and touching).[82]

Competent teaching is crucial to the spiritual health and numerical growth of the church. We will be hard-pressed to grow our churches if we struggle to communicate the things of God's Word. Therefore, we must not forget the other half of our calling, which is to teach. In fact, the Bible states in 1 Timothy 3:2 that the pastor must be "able to teach" (ESV). The phrase "able to teach" is a translation of the Greek word *didaktikos*, which means "skillful at teaching."[83]

The Rationale for Multisensory Preaching

Learning begins with the senses. They are the gateway to the brain. This is why when it comes to biblical teaching, the senses cannot be ignored, because they are vital to learning. And with the knowledge that ADD and ADHD affect the brain and the way it functions and operates, engaging multiple senses at one time would enhance and maximize the learning opportunity for someone with the disease. When it comes to communication, people receive sensory information from the teacher in the form of hearing, seeing, and touching and then transmit that sensory information to the brain for processing.

The role of the senses in learning is not only supported by neurology but also by theology. Three primary senses interface with teaching: hearing, seeing, and touching. Scripture addresses each

Dr. Jason Whitehurst

one in 1 John 1:1, which says, "That which was from the beginning, which we have heard, which we have seen with our eyes, which we have looked at and our hands have touched" (ESV). What John was saying was that they learned from Jesus by seeing Him, hearing Him, and touching Him.

God Himself is a multisensory communicator. If you look at God's general revelation to man, God teaches us about Himself from what we hear, see, touch, smell, and taste. This is what is referred to as natural revelation, as God reveals Himself to mankind through nature. The multisensory nature of the creation captivates our attention, helps clarify our understanding of God, and is absolutely unforgettable.

When you see a sunset, you realize God created the sun and it reveals how powerful He is. When you hear the first cry of your newborn baby, you realize God created that precious infant in His image. When you smell the salt of the ocean or the fresh scent of roses, you realize God created the ocean and the plants and they are a work of His hand. What humans can perceive in all of nature and creation through seeing, hearing, smelling, touching, and tasting reveal how great God is that He created everything ex nihilo, which means "out of nothing."

Jesus was a multisensory teacher and communicator. Few teachers relied on the power of multisensory teaching more than Jesus. What is seen today in terms of multisensory teaching is not so much a revolution as it is a revival. Jesus used vines, branches, coins, water, wheat, wheat fields, children, and all sorts of visual aids to graphically communicate divine truth.[84]

The Bible Is the Centerpiece of Multi-Sensory Preaching

This brings us to an important reason for careful planning: ensuring that the message of the Bible is the central focus of the weekend services. Visuals can be illuminating. Videos can move and inspire. Lights and props and drama can keep people interested. But too much of a good thing can quickly distract from the very reason people need to be there, which is to apply the Word of God to their lives.

Multisensory preaching by nature does not seek to change the message, only the method of delivery. It is designed to make the message more captivating, more understandable, and more memorable. The communication world is constantly in change, and we must be able to adapt our methods (not the message) to that context. The world of communication has transitioned from no technology to radio, television, computers, and the Internet.[85]

The Intellectual Stimulation of Multisensory Preaching

There also appears to be a prevailing wind of "anti-intellectualism" among many contemporary preachers. This mind-set insinuates that the people in our audiences do not have the intellectual capacity to comprehend mentally challenging content. As a result, some contemporary pastors tone down the theological and cognitive content of their teaching. I heard one popular speaker say he keeps his content on a seventh-grade level. He was applauded.[86]

The problem with this thinking is that it limits the theological growth of church members and also hinders and places restrictions on their relationship with God. Going a step further, it implies to the world that Christians lack the capacity to think, reason, and engage in mentally stimulating thought. Christianity then comes across as a simplistic, mindless, emotional, and nonintellectual faith.[87]

Engaging the audience through intellectual stimulation is a clear advantage of multisensory preaching and communicating for those with ADD. If a person is mentally stimulated by the message or talk being presented, then spans of inattention or lack of focus would decrease by nature.

The Preparation for Multisensory Preaching

Pastors and communicators may read this and feel overwhelmed about transitioning to multisensory preaching or communicating. They see the need for it and how it can be really effective in reaching ADD congregants but are not sure how to start. The transition may look daunting. C. E'Jon Moore says, "If people are like me, when they read something dynamic and new, they want to implement everything they have read right away, to the detriment of the hearer (and their own style of preaching, which needs time to adapt)."[88] Moore highlights that pastors are to start small and utilize creative teams if possible or available, so that the pastor or communicator does not feel the burden to create a message or talk that is multisensory all on his own.

The Presentation of Multisensory Preaching

There are three words to remember when presenting or delivering a multisensory message: attention, comprehension, and retention. Attention means the pastor or communicator gets it. Comprehension means that the audience gets it. And retention means that the audience will never forget it.[89] These are the three key elements that will make the presentation effective. They are essential in multisensory preaching. Comprehension and retention are especially significant for the purpose of this project, because they deal with presenting a message or talk in a way that the person with ADD gets and understands the message, and taking it a step further, that they never forget the message. If a pastor or communicator can incorporate these elements and present with these in mind, he will be highly effective in preaching or communicating to ADD congregants.

In the first five minutes, the ultimate fate of the message will be decided. It is in the first five minutes that the message or talk either takes off or crashes and burns. There must be a solid introduction, either with a video clip or some other method that grabs the attention of the audience.[90] A solid, highly visual introduction will increase the effectiveness of the comprehension and retention aspects of the message.

There are many resources online and in Christian bookstores where a pastor or communicator can purchase attention-grabbing video clips or animations. Bluefish.tv is one example of a website with lots of videos.

The Effectiveness of One-Point Preaching

The one-point preaching model is a way of preaching that breaks a conventional preaching style of three points and a poem. One-point preaching strives to present one main idea or concept that the listener will take home. Andy Stanley, a nondenominational pastor of North Point Community Church, one of the largest and best-known churches in America, is one of the forerunners of this style of preaching. He says that every time he gets up to preach, he wants to take one simple truth and lodge it in the hearts of the listeners. He wants them to know one thing, and what to do with that one thing.[91] Andy Stanley is considered by church members and other communicators and pastors as one of the most effective communicators in the church today.

Stanley discusses the one-point preaching model and says there are two keys to this approach. The first thing for the pastor to know is the one thing he or she wants the audience to know. The second thing the pastor must understand is what the audience should do with that one thing. Instead of having two, three, or four ideas to leave with an audience, a pastor or communicator needs to just pick one.

The process of developing a one-point message or talk is to find the one, build everything around it, and make it stick. The pastor or communicator has to go through the process of discovering or finding the one thing, the one point, he wants to drive home. Once that point is discovered, then the pastor or communicator is to orient the entire message around that one central point or concept. Then after building the message, he has to be able to make it stick.[92] This is accomplished with some sort of illustration, personal story, video clip—something unforgettable. If the one point is simple enough and is catchy, it will stick.

This type of preaching or communicating is effective for ADD congregants because all they have to focus on and understand is one point. The one point is very clear, very well defined, and everything about the message or talk is geared to emphasize the one point. Those with short attention spans can greatly benefit from having to focus on only one general idea. It is the responsibility of the pastor or communicator to make that one idea stick. This is done by using a clear, succinct takeaway that any person can remember. The takeaway will be driving home the one point.

In order to effectively communicate in one-point preaching, the pastor or communicator must internalize the message or talk. In other words, he must own it. What is meant by the pastor or communicator owning the message is that he is able to sit down at a table and communicate the talk to a group of two people in a way that is both conversational and authentic. When a pastor or communicator can tell the sermon rather than just preaching it, he is ready to communicate.

The one-point preaching or communicating style will engage the audience with the text. The message or talk should be presented in such a way that the audience is captivated by it, including being engaged with the Word of God. This is accomplished changing the rate of speed in which the pastor or communicator speaks. It is also accomplished by "slowing down in the curves," which means to take critical turns and material in the message slowly for more effect before speeding back up again.[93]

ADD congregants can benefit greatly from this style of preaching and communicating. Not only can they benefit from it, but the pastor or communicator can as well. Instead of having to put together a nice three- or four-point outline with points and subpoints, the pastor just needs one point, one thought, one concept and then to build the entire sermon or talk around it, own it, and present it.

Endnotes:

1. Dwight E. Stevenson and Charles F. Diehl, Reaching People from the Pulpit: A Guide to Effective Sermon Delivery (New York: Harper, 1958), 4.
2. Ibid.
3. Ibid., 19–23.
4. Ibid., 19.
5. Robinson, Biblical Preaching: The Development and Delivery of Expository Messages, 21.
6. Ibid., 23.
7. Ibid., 26.
8. Ibid., 27.
9. Ibid., 28.
10. Rick Blackwood, The Power of Multi-Sensory Preaching and Teaching: Increase Attention, Comprehension, and Retention, location 128–29.
11. Ibid., location 978–89.
12. Ibid., location 1006.
13. Ibid., location 1310.
14. Ibid., location 1342.
15. Ibid., location 1440.
16. Ibid., location 1452.
17. Rick Blackwood, The Power of Multi-Sensory Preaching and Teaching: Increase Attention, Comprehension, and Retention, by C. E'Jon Moore. The Christian Manifesto Review, February

22, 2012, http://thechristianmanifesto.com/archives/book-review/the-power-of-multisensory-preaching-and-teaching.
18. Blackwood, The Power of Multisensory Preaching and Teaching: Increase Attention, Comprehension, and Retention, location 2547
19. Ibid., location 2579.
20. Stanley and Jones, Communicating for a Change, 12.
21. Ibid., 106.
22. Ibid., 157.

Chapter 4
Counseling Effectively Those with ADD and ADHD

The field of counseling and psychology is so broad that a chapter on counseling could easily turn into a book about counseling. There is no lack of valuable sources to be found concerning the large field of psychology. Churches are living in a time when there are more books, journal articles, essays, magazines, and websites that deal with psychology and mental and social disorders than ever before. The wealth of knowledge that can be gained from these sources for pastors and ministers is great but also overwhelming, because there is simply so much.

With this in mind, the purpose of this chapter is to focus on a specific aspect of counseling, which is to help pastors and ministers effectively counsel those who have ADD or ADHD. The purpose of this chapter is not to be exhaustive but to provide some fundamentals and establish framework for pastors in ministering and counseling those in the church who have the disease.

Dr. Jason Whitehurst

Pastors counsel with church members all the time. Pastors and ministers do premarital counseling, family counseling, spiritual-growth counseling, soul care, and other forms of counseling. Pastors and ministers need to be aware that a church member they are counseling has ADD or ADHD, because that knowledge, along with understanding ADD, should enable the pastor or minister to counsel more effectively.

The aim is not to make pastors or ministers licensed professionals but to provide concepts and applications that will make the counseling, which they already do or will do, more effective. Pastor and ministers are already counseling as a part of their pastoral duties. It is the hope of the author that, after reading this thesis project, they will recognize those who have ADD or ADHD and be more effective at counseling with them.

It should be stated that any time a pastor or minister is counseling a church member and the problems are deeper than what a pastor or minister is capable of helping with, he should make a referral to a licensed professional and not try to do something he is incapable of doing or does not have the knowledge to do.

Understanding ADD and Twenty-First-Century Christian Counseling

The pressing concern at the inception of the twenty-first century is that people are hurting and searching frantically for hope and a new life. If there is ever a time for godly leadership, servanthood, and biblical counsel, it is now.[94]

May I Have Your Attention Please?

Sadly, there is a lack of adequate treatment. Over the last several decades, research studies have repeatedly proven the efficacy of counseling. Moreover, religious and faith-based psychotherapy have skyrocketed, showing again and again the great value that ensues when faith meets counseling. What is sad is the gap between persons needing help and the lack of trained individuals available to provide quality care.[95] There is a great divide between Christian clients and the number of mental health professionals available to give care. The idea of finding a Christian counselor in the twenty-first century seems problematic.

Dr. Tim Clinton says, concerning twenty-first century Christian counseling,

> Christian counseling and pastoral care is grounded upon the centrality of healing relationships with both vertical and horizontal dimensions. Like all counseling, it is dyadic in its horizontal dimension between at least two persons. As truly Christian counseling, it becomes uniquely triadic due to God's presence in the vertical, supernatural dimension. In Christian counseling, the Holy Spirit is the third person in every counseling situation. Since this vertical dimension is unique to Christian counseling, it is essential that we begin healing pursuits with the relational God-with Father, Son, and Holy Spirit.[96]

Christian counseling, then, may be defined as a triadic healing encounter with the living Christ, facilitated by a helper who assists this redemptive, healing process, helping another get unstuck and moving forward on the path to spiritual maturity and psycho-social-emotional health.[97] Dr. Clinton also states that Christian counseling has to be more about caring than curing. The focus must be more on caring for those that are hurting and not just trying to cure those that are hurting.

Dr. Clinton concludes the state of affairs in twenty-first century Christian counseling by saying,

> Christian counseling is wonderful, maddening, joyous work. Those called to walk with and serve the hurting are sometimes overwhelmed, often confused, and occasionally avoidant of walking committedly in this calling. We understand this because we ourselves know this joy and are beset, at times, with these very same struggles. The wonder of it all is that Jesus sends the Spirit—all the time and in every way—to comfort us and to set us free of ourselves. Truly, our real life—and that of our clients and parishioners—is hidden with Christ in God. If we look for it, He always reveals it.[98]

In light of the current climate for Christian counseling in the twenty-first century, it is imperative that pastors and ministers step up and do what they can to effectively counsel their parishioners. It is not solely the responsibility of mental health professionals or Christian counselors. The call is not for pastors to go above or beyond what they are capable but for pastors and ministers to do what they can, to put forth the effort to a hurting world. More specifically, for the purpose of this project, to those in their congregations who suffer from ADD or ADHD.

Understanding ADD and Coexisting Conditions

Before a pastor or minister can begin to effectively counsel, or attempt to counsel, with someone who has ADD or ADHD, he needs to be aware that more may be going on than what appears on the surface. A pastor or minister may be aware that a church member has ADD, but what he may not know is that there are coexisting conditions with the ADD.

A person with ADD is six times more likely to have another mental disorder than most other people. ADD or ADHD usually overlaps with other disorders. ADD has an extremely high rate of comorbidity with virtually every mental disease listed in the DSM-IV.[99] Comorbidity is a medical term used to describe other disorders that are present with ADD. For example, if someone has ADD or ADHD and manic depression, the manic depression is considered comorbid.[100]

Among the most common coexisting conditions are mood disorders. Mood disorders, such as depression, now referred to as dysthymia, and manic depression, referred to as bipolar disorder, occur in about 25 percent of people who have ADD.[101] Sometimes, ADD is mistaken for bipolar disorder.

ADD is complicated, which is why pastors and ministers should not treat church members who may have more complex problems than a pastor's area of knowledge and expertise allows him to counsel. Church members with ADD are not to be counseled lightly.

There needs to be consideration of a referral, and the pastor or minister needs to recognize his own limitations.

Understanding ADD and Connecting

One of the most dynamic ways ministers can be effective in their counseling of ADD or ADHD congregants is simply connecting with them. Referring back to the symptoms of ADD and ADHD, because of the disorder and the symptoms that go along with the disease, those with ADD or ADHD often struggle in relationships. Because they are misunderstood or simply cannot be tolerated by other human beings, those with ADD and ADHD often do not have the quality in their relationships that people without the disease have. By simply connecting, building a relationship, a pastor or minister has already begun the process for effective counseling.

Ordinary people have the power to change other people's lives. The power is found in connection, the profound meeting when the truest part of one soul meets the emptiest parts in another and finds something there. When that happens, the giver is left more full than before and the receiver is less afraid, usually eager to experience an even deeper and more mutual connection.[102]

The power to meaningfully change lives does not reside on giving good advice, though counseling plays a part for certain. It does not depend on insight, though having self-awareness that disrupts complacency and points toward new understanding is important. But the power to meaningfully change lives depends on connecting, on bringing two people into an experience of shared life.[103]

May I Have Your Attention Please?

A pastor or minister may read this project and say that he is not good at counseling, he is not adequately trained, or he feels inferior or has a limited vocabulary and is not able to explain concepts or engage in dialogue with someone who is struggling with issues. But what that pastor can do is make a connection. Even the most ordinary and untrained pastor or minister can establish that meaningful relationship with a congregant so that effective counseling will take place.

Understanding ADD and Coaching

Coaching is a new form of treatment of ADD that is growing in popularity. Many health-care professionals are only somewhat knowledgeable about coaching as it pertains to ADD or ADHD. There is an increased demand for coaching as a treatment for ADD because of its apparent effectiveness. The increased demand for ADHD coaching comes from the fact that most adults who struggle with ADD or ADHD would like nothing more than to make adjustments that will change their lives for the better. The problem with that is the follow through, which is where coaches can help.

The way that coaching works is that there is a coach-patient relationship that is goal driven. The coach actively works with the ADD sufferer to create practical strategies to enhance his or her life. Coaches begin by helping them identify their goals and then devising a game plan for achieving those goals.

Coaching is highly individualized, and for this reason, there is no standard method used by all coaches. Coaches must be able to create custom strategies that relate to the abilities and challenges each one of their members faces to bring about positive change.

Coaching is different from other forms of counseling and behavior treatment in that it is not philosophy driven but is goal oriented. Coaches are much more hands on than a traditional counselor might be. Coaches will give honest assessments to the people they work with who have ADD, and sometimes even tough love. They will give them reminders, motivation, and gauge their progress as those with ADD reach for their goals. For example, a coach may call the person he is working with and ask if the person paid his or her bills or did some other task he or she was supposed to complete. Coaching is extremely hands on and is about accountability, which is what those with ADD are showing a desire for.[104]

Coaching does have its limits. It can help those who have ADD and need help setting goals and accomplishing tasks. It serves well as an accountability form of treatment as well. Where coaching is not effective is dealing with those who have ADD and suffer from serious mental and psychological issues that need more extensive treatment than setting goals and being held accountable. Coaching is an effective form of treatment for those who do not have issues that demand more clinical approaches to treatment.

A pastor that has been trained and understands ADD or ADHD can be a coach. He can help sufferers set goals. He can be hands on with them, giving them honest assessments of where they are in their progress. He can help to hold them accountable in reaching their goals. Coaching is a form of ADD treatment through counseling that is highly effective. Coaching does require a good amount of time from the pastor. Time is the area where a pastor will have to discern whether or not coaching someone with ADD would be a detraction from his ministry because of the amount of time coaching takes. A viable, and possibly better, option would be for a pastor to get a professional counselor involved to do the coaching, so that the pastor does not absorb all of his time into one individual.

Coaching is actually an area that pastors can excel at. Pastors are called to be shepherds, to hold people accountable every day, to cast a church vision, to set church goals, and to give an honest assessment of where the church is in relation to those goals. All of these things that pastors do on a regular basis can be transposed on an individual level and coach those ADD congregants who need the help.

Just as with connecting, these are ways that any pastor can be effective. They do not have to take seminary courses on how to connect with an individual and disciple him or her. Pastors and ministers do not need extensive training on how to be a good accountability partner, which really is what coaching is—a form of an accountability partner. These are methods of being effective with ADD congregants that do not require much training. They just require a pastor who is willing to take the time to connect, or take the time to coach.

Dr. Jason Whitehurst

Understanding an Integrative Model for Pastors

Pastors are theologians. They seek to relate, in an individually fitting manner, the healing and liberating message of the gospel to their parishioners' life history. In the past, this role model reigned relatively uncontested: pastors would speak primarily as theologians, whether as liturgists, preachers, religious counselors, or father confessors. In late modernity, by contrast, pastors are confronted with the reproach that in communicating with their clients/parishioners, their competence has changed from theology to psychology.[105]

In the integrative model, Stefan Gartner proposes a model in which a pastor is able to act as a theologian and a psychologist. In other words, the pastor or minister is still able to speak about theology in a counseling setting but also able to use terms used in psychology. Gartner feels that the problem with pastors today is that in counseling settings they have become so consumed with the psychological aspect that they neglect the theological aspect of pastoral counseling.

Basically he is stating that pastors who are counseling are trying too much to act like clinical psychologists rather than act like pastors who happen to be counseling. His main thrust is that a pastor can remain true to the theological aspect of pastoring and counseling and also speak in psychological terms. It does not have to be one or the other; it can be both with the integrative model. Gartner says that pastor must be "multilingual," or at least "bilingual."

What is meant by that is that a pastor or minister can speak in both theological and psychological terms in a counseling session. Gartner writes,

> To summarize our result, the tension between psychological and theological language games can be resolved once both are recognized as complementary in view of adequately accounting for the multilevel reality experienced and presented by the parishioner: "Both languages would be seen as trying to give shape and meaning to a particular set of human experiences, but they would be doing so in different ways."[106]

What does the integrative model mean for pastors? What can be gleaned from it? The answer is that pastors and ministers do not need to get so wrapped in trying to be clinical when they are counseling ADD church members that they neglect their role as pastor or minister to speak theological truths. A pastor or minister can wear both hats at the same time and can speak in both theological and psychological terms in the same session.

Understanding ADD and Positive Psychology

Another even more recent advance in the behavioral sciences that can be helpful in pastoral ministry and formation is positive psychology. The discipline of positive psychology is about living well. It is about accentuating the positive things and not focusing as much on the negative aspects or issues. Its goal is to encourage the field of clinical psychology not to see itself as merely being a "repair shop" for emotional difficulties (as important as this role is) but also to help people uncover their signature strengths. By drawing attention to people's gifts, talents, and virtues, people can then build upon what is good instead of solely focusing on correcting what is problematic.[107]

According to Martin Seligman, initiator of the contemporary positive psychology movement,

> The field of positive psychology at the subjective level is about positive subjective experience: well-being and satisfaction (past); joy, the sensual pleasures, and happiness (present); and constructive cognitions about the future-optimism, hope, and faith. At the individual level it is about positive personal traits- the capacity for love and vocation, courage, interpersonal skill, aesthetic sensibility, perseverance, forgiveness, originality, future-mindedness, high talent, and wisdom ... Psychology is not just the study of disease, weakness, and damage; it also is the study of strength and virtue. Treatment is not just fixing what is wrong; it is also building what is right ... the major strides in prevention have largely come from a perspective focused on systematically building competency, not correcting weakness This, then, is the general stance of positive psychology toward prevention. It claims that there is a set of buffers against psychopathology: the positive human traits.[108]

Positive psychology is not a concealer but a way for people to look at their situation in a different light and be freed from all the negative focus they may have. This is beneficial not only to the person being counseled with, but also it is practical for the pastor or minister to apply in his own life.

May I Have Your Attention Please?

This is beneficial for the person who suffers from ADD or ADHD because it promotes an optimistic outlook on his or her situation. Instead of focusing on all the hindrances and life changes that have to be made and how they affect day-to-day living in a negative way, the point is took at the glass half full. Yes, there is a real condition that the ADD/ADHD sufferer has to deal with, but focus on the positive things like how treatment can enable a normal life.

Understanding ADD and Biblical Therapy

Biblical therapy is a newer method of helping those in need of counseling. It is controversial, to say the least. Here are some quotes about the controversial nature of biblical therapy and what it is exactly:

> This is a controversial form of counseling by pastors and church leaders. It created a stir in 2005 when Southern Baptist Seminary announced a total change, that they were moving from the "pastoral counseling" to the "Biblical counseling."[109]

> "All aspects of our lives—including our spiritual, moral, and psychological—are to be informed and governed by the application of and obedience to Holy Scripture. In this therapeutic culture ... physicians and counselors often ignore human sin and its effects, neglect our most fundamental human and spiritual needs, and therefore misunderstand our condition, mistreat our problems, and sometimes unintentionally do more harm than good." The resolution calls on SBC churches "to reclaim practical biblical wisdom,

Christ-centered counseling, and the restorative ministry of the care and cure of souls."[110]

In essence, the school was saying that it was opposed to integrating the practice of secular counseling and psychology and blending it with scriptures. That combination is the pastoral counseling model. They were in favor of using only the Bible, not any secular methods or concepts, to counsel with.

There has been debate between those who are for pastoral counseling and those who oppose it in favor of biblical counseling. Those who are advocates of biblical therapy would say to a person with ADD or ADHD, "Remember Philippians 4:13: You can do all things through Christ who strengthens you." They may also quote passages on faith and believing and trusting in God, that He will not put more on you that you are able to withstand and that faith moves the hand of God in your situation.

Those who are in favor of pastoral counseling said it would be an error to ignore what has been discovered through secular findings concerning disorders, and that it is unfair to the person being counseled or treated.[111]

Pastors and ministers have to decide which side of the fence they are on with this method of counseling. For pastors, they have to make a decision of whether to practice biblical therapy and only use the Bible as their source of information in counseling or use the findings of the world of psychology along with theological concepts and Scripture combined to counsel with. For the purpose of this project, it is being presented because it is an issue that each pastor and minister has to resolve in his heart. In order to be effective in ministering to ADD congregants, a pastor or minister must be clear as to how he approaches counseling.

In summation, there are several ways in which a pastor or minister can effectively counsel someone who has ADD or ADHD and the significance of effective counseling to those congregants. A pastor or minister does not have to have a professional counseling degree to be effective at counseling those with ADD or ADHD; he just has to be willing.

Whether it is through connecting or coaching or using positive psychology or biblical therapy, every pastor can be effective. These methods are practical ways in which ADD congregants can be engaged and soul care can take place.

Endnotes:

1. Timothy E. Clinton et al., Caring for People God's Way: Personal and Emotional Issues, Addictions, Grief, and Trauma, (Nashville, TN: Nelson Reference & Electronic, 2005), 4.
2. Ibid., 8.
3. Ibid., 14–15.
4. Ibid., 15.
5. Ibid., 23.
6. Thomas E. Brown, Attention Deficit Disorder: The Unfocused Mind in Children and Adults (New Haven, CT: Yale University Press, 2006), 200.
7. Edward M. Hallowell and John J. Ratey, Delivered from Distraction: Getting the Most Out of Life with Attention Deficit Disorder (New York, NY: Ballantine Books, 2006), 132.
8. Ibid., 133.
9. Lawrence J. Crabb, Connecting: Healing Ourselves and Our Relationships (Nashville, TN: W Publishing Group, 2005), 31.
10. Ibid.
11. Ibid.
12. Stefan Gartner, "Staying a Pastor while Talking Like a Psychologist? A Proposal for an Integrative Model." Christian Bioethics: Non-Ecumenical Studies in Medical Morality 16, no. 1 (January 2010): 48–60. Academic Search Complete, EBSCOhost (accessed April 11, 2012).
13. Ibid.

14. Robert J. Wicks and Tina C. Buck. "Reframing for Change: The Use of Cognitive Behavioral Therapy and Native Psychology in Pastoral Ministry and Formation." Human Development 32, no. 3 (Fall 2011): 8–14. Education Research Complete, EBSCOhost (accessed April 2, 2012).
15. Ibid.
16. David Winfrey, "Biblical Therapy." Christian Century 124, no. 2 (January 23, 2007): 24. MasterFILE Premier, EBSCOhost (accessed April 2, 2012).
17. Ibid.
18. Ibid.
19. Patricia Bays, "The Care and Nurture of Volunteers." Clergy Journal 82, no. 7 (May 2006): 8–10. Academic Search Complete, EBSCOhost (accessed April 19, 2012).
20. Ibid.
21. Bill Hybels, The Volunteer Revolution: Unleashing the Power of Everybody (Grand Rapids, MI: Zondervan, 2004), 16.
22. Ibid., 17–18.
23. Bill Hybels, "The Seven Myths of Volunteerism," BuildingChurchLeaders (July 11, 2007): page nr., http://www.buildingchurchleaders.com/articles/2006/060403.html (accessed April 19, 2012).
24. Ibid.
25. Ibid.
26. Hybels, The Volunteer Revolution: Unleashing the Power of Everybody, 81–82.

Chapter 5

Training Volunteers to Work Effectively with Those with ADD and ADHD

Churches rely on volunteers. Ministry cannot take place, and churches cannot grow and thrive and be what God would have them to be, without volunteers. Churches can have great staffs, but if they do not have volunteers to help support the ministry, more than likely it is not going to be very fruitful and productive. Churches depend on volunteers to keep their ministries and programs running.[112] Christians have a powerful call to offer their gifts to strengthen and build the community of faithful people and to help that community reach out to others in loving service. By their baptism, Christians are called to work together to bring the good news of God in Christ to a hurting world.[113]

The fact is that if churches want to be successful in having a healthy volunteer culture that effectively ministers to ADD or ADHD congregants, the church must be recruiting, equipping, coaching, and retaining these volunteers. Volunteerism does not happen by accident,

May I Have Your Attention Please?

but it is a product of the vision of the church and the culture in place. Bill Hybels writes in his book *The Volunteer Revolution* that church members need to be given the opportunity to go from "spectator to participator."[114] Hybels goes on to say that when people are given the opportunity to serve as volunteers in the local church, they are thrilled to be able to serve and find volunteering extremely satisfying.

He cites one e-mail that says,

> Three years ago you challenged me to get involved as a volunteer. I was hesitant at first, but you wouldn't let up. Now I can't thank you enough. The meaning I derive, the sense of ownership I feel, the friendships I have built, the spiritual growth I've experienced—it's all directly related to finding my niche in serving. I will be grateful to you for the rest of my life for inviting me into the game.[115]

Hybels continues that he gets these kinds of e-mails and letters all the time: people are genuinely thrilled and grow spiritually through volunteerism. He writes that people find their place, where they fit, and as a result, they find meaning in their lives they did not experience before.

The purpose of this chapter is to show misconceptions about volunteers, the reasons for volunteering, recruiting volunteers, equipping volunteers, and coaching volunteers that can effectively understand, teach, and lead congregants who have ADD or ADHD. The goal is that this chapter will give pastors, ministers, and church leaders a practical guide to get these volunteers in their churches and to get them an understanding of what ADD is and how they can be a part of ministering to those who have the disease, whereas previously they may not have been engaged or reached.

Misconceptions about Volunteers

Every church has, at some time or another, complained about a lack of volunteers. Excuses are given as to why volunteers aren't showing up and a mad scramble usually ensues to figure out how to get the work of the church done. But most of the conceptions that we have about volunteers are misconceptions. Some of the reasons our churches give for not making great strides in recruiting volunteers are not good reasons ... they're myths. Here are the seven most common myths about volunteers, as discussed by Bill Hybels in an article he wrote.[116]

The first myth is that there are not enough volunteers to go around. There are plenty of volunteers to go around. It is the job of the pastor or minster to find out why the people are not serving and get them back in the game. It is not because a lack of people to serve, but there is a reason, and it must be identified. To find out the reason, poll people, ask questions, do surveys to see why people are not volunteering. Do some research within your church. It will not take long to identify the reasons.

The second myth is volunteers are only capable of doing the busy work of the church. By this, Hybels is referring to the repetitive tasks that the staff does not want to do.[117] This is false. Volunteers are capable of doing much more than they are often assigned, and

May I Have Your Attention Please?

one reason they quit is because they are not reaching their full volunteer potential.

The third myth identified by Hybels is that volunteers are free help. They are technically not paid, but volunteers are not to be viewed as free help. Churches are to invest into their volunteers resources, training, and competent leadership.

The fourth myth listed about volunteer is that volunteers want to serve in one role for a lifetime. Once again, this is false. It is not uncommon for, three to six months into a role, a volunteer to start self-assessing if they are in the right role or not.

The fifth myth discussed is volunteers are not interested in training or development. Hybels states he finds the opposite to be true. Volunteers want to be the best at their job, not subpar. Volunteers want to be trained. They want workshops and seminars which will enable them to be more effective in their areas of ministry. They want to be well equipped to do the job they volunteered for.

The sixth myth brought to light is that volunteers need encouragement from heaven but they do not really need encouragement from people on earth. Hybels instructs his staff that they are to be constantly lighting the fires and fanning the flames of the passions of volunteers. He says if you want to lead in a volunteer revolution, you have to have an inspired culture, and that is an unstoppable force. You fan the flames by offering verbal praise. You fan the flames and light fires by recognizing people for their efforts. You make them feel like they are the most important people to the ministry. You give them tasks and assignments that are

Dr. Jason Whitehurst

not too easy that they become bored with them, but you challenge them and maximize their gifts and abilities. These things will keep volunteers stoked.

The seventh myth exposed is that volunteerism is all output and no return. About this myth, Hybels states,

> Volunteerism done right, volunteerism done biblically, wisely, and in the power of the Holy Spirit will not diminish the quality of a person's life. It will do precisely the opposite! Volunteerism done right will dramatically and often radically, positively transform a person's life. Inviting a person into servant hood in the cause of Christ is often one of the kindest, most life giving, joy-producing, spiritually-enriching opportunities you can offer somebody.[118]

Hybels is a firm believer that volunteers are greatly rewarded and to serve is a great honor and privilege. His premise is that there is a joy and satisfaction that comes from being in service to the local church. I have heard interviews with him, and he talks about multimillionaire businessmen who have so much earthly success, but they tell Hybels that the favorite part of their week is when they get to volunteer in the children's area. Or they get to work the food pantry.

Now that these myths have been exposed, pastors do not have an excuse not to pursue members of their church to volunteer. There should be no hesitation or shying away from asking someone to serve as a volunteer.

The Reasons for Volunteerism

Jesus recognized the importance of volunteering. Jesus trained, equipped, and motivated the ordinary people around Him to do extraordinary things. Jesus motivated those around Him to serve and use their human capabilities to do unbelievable things.

The life of a disciple, or follower of Christ, is a life of service. The disciples got to serve the food at the feeding of the five thousand. They were able to take part in the greatest miracle recorded. It is called the greatest miracle Jesus performed because it involved the most number of people and all four gospels include it.

In the book of Acts, the deacons were meant to be servants. Deacons were to wait tables and serve the widows and see to the needs of others. Being a deacon was not some prestigious title that was flaunted like it is in today's churches where there are men who feel because they are a deacon they have arrived. That is not the original intent of deacons. Deacons from the onset of the early church were meant to be volunteers and to serve.

Another reason is found in Ephesians 4:11–13. The apostle Paul writes, "And he gave the apostles, the prophets, the evangelists, the shepherds and teachers, to equip the saints for the work of ministry, for building up the body of Christ, until we all attain to the unity of the faith and of the knowledge of the Son of God, to mature manhood, to the measure of the stature of the fullness of Christ" (ESV).

Believers are given an exhortation from Paul to work to "equip the saints" and that the body of Christ would be built up and unified.

Dr. Jason Whitehurst

Through being a volunteer in the local church, a Christian is fulfilling his or her obligation to heed this word from Paul that God would be glorified and His kingdom would be advanced on the earth. It is the responsibility of every believer, not just the pastor or minister or staff person.

Another reason found in Scripture is that it is better to serve than be served. The Bible records in Acts 20:35, "In all things I have shown you that by working hard in this way we must help the weak and remember the words of the Lord Jesus, how he himself said, 'It is more blessed to give than to receive'" (ESV). It is better to serve and freely give than to receive service, as a Christian.

Yet another biblical mandate to volunteer and serve others is in Galatians 6:9–10, which reads, "And let us not grow weary of doing good, for in due season we will reap, if we do not give up. So then, as we have opportunity, let us do good to everyone, and especially to those who are of the household of faith" (ESV).

The clear command here, written by Paul, is to serve those who are fellow brothers and sisters in the faith as Christians. Also, do not get tired of volunteering or serving but continue even in tiresome times, because those who continue in service will reap the rewards of being faithful in their serving.

The Bible also states in 1 Peter 4:10, "As each has received a gift, use it to serve one another, as good stewards of God's varied grace" (ESV). Once again, the concept of volunteerism—using one's abilities and gifts to serve the local church body—is seen in Scripture. There is clearly a scriptural mandate to be serving as a volunteer in the local church that the body of Christ might be edified and the one serving would be fulfilling what God has equipped and called him or her to do.

A God-given passion, an area of intense interest, is buried inside each Christian. One of the goals of volunteering is to discover that passion. Connecting one's spiritual gift or gifts with an area of passion is the key to ultimate effectiveness and fulfillment in serving.[119] This is also one of the keys in maintaining the energy to volunteer, because when you serve in an area you are passionate about, you do not have to be fired up to stay involved or engaged. You cannot help but to show up and volunteer.

Recruiting Volunteers

Pastors should identify and recruit those who could be effective in serving congregants with ADD. For example, a pastor would not want to recruit anyone who does not have patience, compassion, or tolerance.

Recruiting should start with planning. The areas or ministries which need volunteers must be identified by the pastor or minister or a committee or staff.[120] There also may be ministries that the pastor or staff would like to start and will need volunteers for. All of this can be hashed out in the planning phase of the recruiting process. In order to know the people that are needed, it is helpful to know what areas they are needed in, because they will help weed out volunteers who will not fit a particular ministry or area of the church.

The next step is to create a job description for the position that is to be filled. The job description should be specific and thorough and should also provide the expectations for the position so that a volunteer understands what is required of them. Volunteers will likely last longer if they know upfront what is expected of them, who they report to, and what kind of commitment they are signing up for.

One thing I highly recommend for each church is to have a ministry manual that lists all the positions in the church that are filled by volunteers. It should be exhaustive and include every position from nursery worker to sound tech. Each job should have a detailed outline of job responsibilities and duties and the qualifications a person needs to fill the position. A prospective volunteer should be given a copy of the position you are recruiting him for so he is fully aware of all the dynamics and parameters involved in the position he will fill.

There should also be qualifications for a volunteer. Quite honestly, everyone who desires to be a volunteer should not necessarily be allowed to serve. First and foremost, each volunteer must have a personal, authentic relationship with Jesus Christ. Second, a volunteer must be willing to commit to serving for a specific amount of time, normally ranging from one to three years, depending on the role or position. If need be, based on the person, the position, and the situation, a trial period of six months may be needed to make sure the position is a good fit for the volunteer and the church.

Third, a volunteer should have a desire or passion to serve in the area he or she is placed. Fourth, a volunteer must be willing to submit to all authoritative figures, as well as attend scheduled meetings for the ministry area. Fifth, a volunteer must be willing to attend all training seminars or workshops that pertain to the area of service. There are other qualifications that a church may have, but these are the qualifications that are fairly basic and general across the board for many churches.

In the recruiting process, do not beg a volunteer for help. By doing this, what is being said to the volunteers is that they are being asked to jump on a sinking ship.[121] Some people will join out of guilt and respond to the plea for help. But when people end up serving in a ministry that isn't in line with their gifts and passions, they will likely become frustrated and burned out. Instead of telling people what you need, tell them how you can help them use their gifts and experiences.

What I do with potential volunteers is go to them and have a conversation where I recognize their spiritual gifts and their natural abilities and talents and tell them I feel like they would be a great fit in a particular position. I point out that not only will it be rewarding for the area they serve, but they will be using the spiritual gifts God has given them to edify the church. When you start the conversation with affirmation when recruiting a volunteer, it usually goes much better.

One of the most effective tools in recruiting volunteers is to have a ministry fair.[122] There can be a ministry fair once or twice a year where people from each ministry or department set up tables with information about their ministries or departments and the specific roles or positions that are available to those who would like to serve.

The best thing about the fairs is they give a general overview of all the serving opportunities available in the church. People can stop at a few tables and learn which ministries or areas might fit their gifts and passions. The fairs can also attract people who could be helped by the ministries. It is a win-win situation for those who want to serve and for those who are to be served. The focus of ministry fairs is on those who are not connected or volunteering and looking for ways to serve, and not the specific needs of a ministry or department.

The final stage in the recruiting process is to evaluate prospective volunteers and the ministries they fit into. After having a ministry fair or going to a person one-on-one and giving a personal invitation to volunteer, those involved in the planning process from the beginning need to evaluate each person and how they will fit into the role they are seeking to volunteer in.[123]

Be aware of requirements for screening volunteers. A police check may be required for volunteers working with children and youth. Hospitals have procedures for screening pastoral visitors. Find out about sexual misconduct guidelines in your jurisdiction and make volunteers aware of these. If a police check is required, the congregation should pay the fee on behalf of the volunteer.[124]

Equipping Volunteers

Those in leadership positions often have access to resources and information that would be valuable to volunteers, yet it is not passed along to them. If a pastor or minister has not done so, he needs to create a resource library with any media, documents, reference materials, etc., that would be helpful to volunteer and enable them to be as effective as they can be in the capacity in which they are serving.[125]

This is true in educating and equipping volunteers to be effective in their dealings and encounters with those who have ADD. Whatever resources a pastor or minister has at his disposal should be made available to volunteers, so that they may be equipped to teach or minister to those church members with ADD or ADHD.

All of the information in this chapter is important for volunteers to know. For example, if a volunteer has the information presented, he or she is much less likely to get frustrated or burned out while trying to help those with ADD or ADHD. Just a fundamental understanding can prevent frustration, whereas if the volunteers did not know anything about ADD or ADHD, they may take it personally or just get tired of a situation or person.

A great way to equip volunteers is to let them observe the ministry or area they will serve in. This will give them a better feel for what they are committing to, and they it will answer a lot of the questions they may have inside before they ever get started.[126] This will give volunteers a firsthand look at what it will be like to potentially volunteer in an area or ministry where there are ADD church members.

Volunteers have to be equipped. As Bill Hybels said in his discussion about myths concerning volunteers, they do want training and development.[127] If volunteers are going to teach and lead and serve those with this disease, they are going to need the training on what ADD is, what the symptoms are, whom it affects, and how they as a volunteer can still minister to those congregants.

Coaching Volunteers

Coaching involves mentoring and building a relationship between a person who is more experienced and someone who is less experienced. The individual, who trains the volunteer and is the point person to whom the volunteer reports, is the best option to be the volunteer's coach. Coaches should establish credibility with the volunteers and hold them accountable.

There are three key lessons that are important to note when coaching volunteers. The first lesson is that a new volunteer is a fragile volunteer.[128] A longtime volunteer can handle a mishap, but a new volunteer is much more likely to become discouraged or disillusioned. A volunteer's first ministry experience may determine his attitude toward ministry for the rest of his life. The coach should ask the new volunteer probing questions to see how he or she is doing and help ease any burden or angst he or she may have as a new volunteer. This will alleviate some of the volunteer fallout.

The second lesson to be learned when coaching volunteers is that the easiest way to defeat a volunteer is to waste his or her time. Volunteers are people who are not paid and therefore have other jobs. They have families and other obligations. The best way to get volunteers to quit is to waste their time when a meeting is taking place.

If you schedule a meeting for your volunteers and when they get there you are unprepared, lack organization, don't start on time, and discuss things that are trivial or insignificant, the chances of your volunteers being retained for a long period of time are slim to none.

The third lesson is that volunteers needed to be reminded constantly that what they are doing is not in vain. Volunteers need to hear again and again that what they are doing has significance and value and they are making a difference.[129] This is especially true if a volunteer is dealing with someone with ADD or ADHD, someone who may be inattentive or hyperactive or impulsive. That volunteer needs to know how to get through to them, and that he or she is being effective in getting through to them.

Also, the span of control is an aspect to be considered when leading volunteers. The span of control is the number of people that a leader can effectively be in control of at any one time. No one leader can effectively be in charge of every single volunteer in a ministry, but a leader can effectively have five to six people under him or her.[130]

This number can fluctuate depending on several factors, such as the organizational structure, organization size, the nature of the position, and the skills and abilities of the volunteers. Each church has to look within its structure and each department to determine how the span of control needs to be outlined and implemented so that no leader has so many volunteers that he or she is not able to be effective in guiding and training them. If there is no span of control, it is detrimental to the volunteers as well as to those who lead them.

In conclusion, when a leader is equipped with the right amount of volunteers to manage, and given the material and information to train them with for the job or position that the volunteer will fill, a healthy model will be in place. The end result of a healthy system is effective leaders and productive volunteers, which brings glory to God and edification to His church.

Endnotes:

1. Patricia Bays, "The Care and Nurture of Volunteers." Clergy Journal 82, no. 7 (May 2006): 8–10. Academic Search Complete, EBSCOhost (accessed April 19, 2012).
2. Tony Morgan and Tim Stevens, Simply Strategic Volunteers: Empowering People for Ministry (Loveland, CO: Group, 2005), 17.
3. Ibid., 63.
4. Patricia Bays, "The Care and Nurture of Volunteers." Clergy Journal 82, no. 7 (May 2006): 8–10. Academic Search Complete, EBSCOhost (accessed April 19, 2012).
5. Ibid.
6. Ibid.
7. Morgan and Stevens, Simply Strategic Volunteers: Empowering People for Ministry, 41.
8. Bill Hybels, "The Seven Myths of Volunteerism," Building Church Leaders (July 11, 2007): page nr., http://www.buildingchurchleaders.com/articles/2006/060403.html (accessed April 19, 2012).
9. Hybels, The Volunteer Revolution: Unleashing the Power of Everybody, 113.
10. Ibid., 116.

11. "How Many Employees Should Your Supervisors Manage? | Where Great Workplaces Start." Where Great Workplaces Start | Information and conversation on everything HR, brought to you by ERC. http://greatworkplace.wordpress.com/2010/02/17/how-many-employees-should-your-supervisors-manage/ (accessed June 22, 2012).

Appendix A

Educating Volunteers about ADD and ADHD Workshop

Teacher Outline

I. ADD Education for Volunteers

    A. What ADD Is and Is Not

    B. The Symptoms of ADD

    C. The Statistics on ADD and the Rise in Diagnoses

    D. Causes of ADD

    E. Common Myths about ADD

II. Creating an Environment as Volunteers

    A. The Importance

    B. The Planning

    C. The Multisensory Aspect

III. Teaching Methods for Volunteers

    A. Expository Teaching

    B. Multisensory Teaching

    C. One-Point Teaching

IV. Connecting and Coaching as Volunteers

V. Limitations of Volunteers

    1. Volunteers are not staff and do not have the authority of paid staff.

    2. Volunteers are not paid, so they must be handled differently.

    3. Volunteers do not have the time to commit, as a general rule, as paid staff.

    4. Volunteers are not as adequately trained as staff.

    5. Volunteers are not as available as staff.

6. Volunteers should have expectations and job descriptions, but they must be realistic and not the same as paid staff.

7. Volunteers make a ministry function and should not be taken for granted or overloaded.

8. Volunteers are not professional counselors.

9. Volunteers are usually not seminary trained.

10. Volunteers need constant encouragement and training.

Appendix B

Educating Volunteers about ADD and ADHD Workshop

Handout for Workers

I. I. ADD Education for Volunteers

   A. What ADD Is and Is Not

   1. Attention deficit disorder (ADD) is a general term frequently used to describe individuals who have attention deficit hyperactivity disorder without the hyperactive and impulsive behaviors.

   2. The terms ADD and ADHD are often used interchangeably for both those who do and those who do not have symptoms of hyperactivity and impulsiveness.

   3. Attention deficit hyperactivity disorder (ADHD) is the official name used by the American Psychiatric

Association, and it encompasses hyperactive, impulsive, and/or inattentive behaviors.

4. ADHD is a problem with inattentiveness, overactivity, impulsivity, or a combination. For these problems to be diagnosed as ADHD, they must be out of the normal range.

5. ADHD is one of the most common neurobehavioral disorders of childhood. It is usually first diagnosed in childhood and often lasts into adulthood.

6. There are three different types of ADHD, and the type depends on the strength of the symptoms in each person.

   i. **Predominantly Inattentive Type:** It is hard for the individual to organize or finish a task, to pay attention to details, or to follow instructions or conversations. The person is easily distracted or forgets details of daily routines.

   ii. **Predominantly Hyperactive-Impulsive Type:** The person fidgets and talks a lot. It is hard to sit still for long (e.g., for a meal or while doing homework). Smaller children may run, jump, or climb constantly. The individual feels restless and has trouble with impulsivity. Someone who is impulsive may interrupt others a lot, grab things from people, or speak at inappropriate times. It is hard for the person to wait his or her turn or listen to directions. A person with impulsiveness may have more accidents and injuries than others.

    iii. **Combined Type:** Symptoms of the above two types are equally present in the person.

7. ADD is not simply having some of the symptoms associated with the disease.

8. What determines whether or not it is ADD is the total picture of a person's state and their actions, their intertwined existences, intensities of behavior, and frequencies.

9. Many tendencies and behaviors exhibited in people with ADD also appear in people who do not have the disease. The manifestation of one or another of these traits is not unusual but actually common.

B. The Symptoms of ADD

1. There are more symptoms listed that need to be understood that go beyond just the inability to pay attention or hyperactivity.

2. ADD is defined by the presence or absence of the symptoms set forth in the DSM-IV. The symptoms fall into three categories: lack of attention (inattentiveness), hyperactivity, and impulsive behavior (impulsivity).

3. There are two clusters of symptoms, one describing symptoms of inattention and the other cluster describing symptoms of hyperactivity and impulsivity. To be even considered for a diagnosis, the criteria set forth in cluster 1 and cluster 2 must be met.

4. In cluster 1, six or more of the following symptoms of inattention have to persist for at least six months to a degree that is maladaptive and inconsistent with a developmental level.

Inattention

i. Often fails to give close attention to details or makes careless mistakes in schoolwork, work, or other activities

ii. Often has difficulty sustaining attention in tasks or play activities

iii. Often does not seem to listen when spoken to directly

iv. Often does not follow through on instructions and fails to finish schoolwork, chores, or duties in the workplace (not due to oppositional failure or failure to understand instructions)

v. Often has difficulty organizing tasks and activities

vi. Often avoids, dislikes, or is reluctant to engage in tasks that require sustained mental effort

vii. Often loses things necessary for tasks or activities

viii. Is often easily distracted by extraneous stimuli

ix. Is often forgetful in daily activities

5. In cluster 2, six or more of the following symptoms of hyperactivity and impulsivity have persisted for at least six months to a degree that is maladaptive and inconsistent with developmental level.

Hyperactivity

i. Often fidgets with hands or feet or squirms in seat

ii. Often leaves seat in classroom or other situations in which remaining seated is expected

iii. Often runs about or climbs excessively when it is inappropriate (in adolescents and adults, may be limited to subjective feelings of restlessness)

iv. Often has difficulty playing or engaging in leisure activities quietly

v. Is often "on the go" or acts as if "driven by a motor"

vi. Often talks excessively

Impulsivity

i. Often blurts out answers before questions have been completed

ii. Often has difficulty awaiting his or her turn

iii. Often interrupts or intrudes on others

6. The following behaviors and problems may stem directly from ADHD or may be the result of related adjustment difficulties:

   i. Chronic lateness and forgetfulness

   ii. Anxiety

   iii. Low self-esteem

   iv. Employment problems

v. Difficulty controlling anger

   vi. Impulsiveness

   vii. Substance abuse or addiction

   viii. Poor organization skills

   ix. Procrastination

   x. Low frustration tolerance

   xi. Chronic boredom

   xii. Difficulty concentrating when reading

   xiii. Mood swings

   xiv. Depression

   xv. Relationship problems

7. A patient must have six out of nine symptoms in either cluster to be diagnosed with ADD or ADHD.

8. A positive diagnosis of ADD or ADHD is based on a doctor's ability to recognize the symptoms present, to ascertain and determine the severity and frequency of the symptoms, to qualify the impact the symptoms are having on the person's life, and to verify that the onset of symptoms occurred during childhood through a series of interviews and evaluations.

9. The American Academy of Pediatrics has issued guidelines to bring clarity to the issue of diagnosing children with ADD. The diagnosis is based on very specific symptoms, which must be present in more than one setting.

    i. Children should have at least six attention symptoms or six hyperactivity/impulsivity symptoms, with some symptoms present before age seven.

    ii. The symptoms must be present for at least six months, seen in two or more settings, and not caused by another problem.

    iii. The symptoms must be severe enough to cause significant difficulties in many settings, including home, school, and relationships with peers.

10. Adults with ADD may have had a history of poorer educational performance and were underachievers.

11. They are more likely to belong to a lower income class.

12. They are more likely to end up in divorce.

C. The Statistics on ADD and the Rise in Diagnoses

1. ADHD is more common than doctors may have previously believed, according to a new study from the Mayo Clinic.

2. Roughly 5 to 8 percent of Americans have been diagnosed with ADD.

3. The American Psychiatric Association states in *Diagnostic and Statistical Manual of Mental Disorders* (DSM-IV-TR) that 3 percent to 7 percent of school-aged children have ADHD.

4. It is now known that these symptoms continue into adulthood for about 60 percent of children with ADHD.

5. Translates into 4 percent of the US adult population, or eight million adults.

6. Most of the adults who have ADD or ADHD do not realize it because they have never been diagnosed with it. Few adults are identified or treated for the disease.

7. ADHD afflicts approximately 3 percent to 10 percent of school-aged children, and an estimated 60 percent of those will maintain the disorder into adulthood.

8. There has been a steady increase in the number of diagnoses since 2003.

9. Dr. Russell Barkley has compiled the following statistics concerning ADHD:

    i. A classroom with thirty students will have between one and three children with ADHD.

    ii. Boys are diagnosed with ADHD three times more often than girls.

    iii. Emotional development in children with ADHD is 30 percent slower than in their non-ADD peers. This means that a child who is ten years old will have the emotional development of a seven-year-old and a twenty-year-old will have the emotional maturity of a fourteen-year-old.

    iv. One-fourth of children with ADHD have serious learning disabilities, such as oral expression, listening skills, reading comprehension, and/or math.

    v. 65 percent of children with ADHD exhibit problems in defiance or problems with authority figures. This can include verbal hostility and temper tantrums.

vi. 75 percent of boys diagnosed with ADD/ADHD have hyperactivity.

vii. 60 percent of girls diagnosed with ADD/ADHD have hyperactivity.

viii. 50 percent of children with ADHD experience sleep problems.

ix. Teenagers with ADHD have almost four times as many traffic citations as non-ADD/ADHD drivers. They have four times as many car accidents and are seven times more likely to have a second accident.

x. 21 percent of teens with ADHD skip school on a regular basis, and 35 percent drop out of school before finishing high school.

xi. 45 percent of children with ADHD have been suspended from school at least once.

xii. 30 percent of children with ADHD have repeated a year in school.

D. Causes of ADD

1. The basis for ADD or ADHD is mostly biological, with heredity contributing about 75 percent of the casual factors.

2. The cause is not behavioral in the sense that people with ADD choose to act a certain way. Rather, they are compelled to respond a certain way in a given situation.

3. It may appear on the outside as if they have a choice, but physiologically they do not. What goes on in their brains prompts them to a certain response.

4. ADD is a biological condition many times and is determined by the genes of the parents before birth. These genes are passed down from generation to generation.

5. If both parents have ADHD, the child is more likely to have the genetic predisposition.

6. In addition to genetics, scientists are studying other possible causes and risk factors including brain injury, environmental exposures (e.g., lead), premature delivery, and low birth weight.

7. Research does not support the popularly held views that ADHD is caused by eating too much sugar,

watching too much television, parenting, or social factors, such as poverty or family chaos.

E. Common Myths about ADD

1. Myth #1 is that everyone has the symptoms of ADD and that anyone with average intelligence can overcome these symptoms. The truth is that ADD affects all levels of intelligence to the person suffering from it.

2. Myth #2 is that ADD is a simple problem of being hyperactive or not listening when someone is talking. The truth is ADD is a complex disorder that involves impairments in focus, organization, motivation, emotional modulation, memory, and other functions of the brain's management system.

3. Myth #3 is that ADD is just a lack of willpower. People with ADD focus on things that interest them; they could focus on other tasks if they really wanted to. The truth is that ADD has nothing to do with willpower, even though it may appear that way. ADD is a brain-chemical problem.

II. Creating an Environment as Volunteers

   A. The Importance

      1. If an environment is created and structured in a way to meet the needs of those with ADD, the rest of the group would also benefit from the structure and elements in place.

      2. A proper environment will lead to spiritual growth in ADD congregants.

      3. A proper environment will lead to church growth numerically.

      4. If an environment is not created, those with ADD are likely to find a place that does meet their needs.

      5. Five elements that should be present in the environment created by volunteers are that it is celebrative, friendly, expectant, relaxed, and positive.

   B. The Planning

      1. "If you fail to plan, you plan to fail."

      2. It has to be intentional. It usually will not occur by accident.

3. The plan should be established and passed down to volunteers from church leadership.

4. All volunteers should be on the same page with the same vision and plan.

5. Volunteers should have the freedom to make suggestions for changes they feel are needed based on what they see occurring.

C. The Multisensory Aspect

1. There are other tools and resources that can be used in a group gathering to engage multiple senses at one time to create an environment that is effective for ADD people.

2. When what is going on in the environment engages more than just one sense, it helps to offset some of the tendencies and symptoms of ADD.

3. The first such resource is PowerPoint or visual media.

4. Using video clips is a great tool to grab the attention of those with ADD or ADHD.

5. Lighting is used to set the mood for an environment. Depending on what the objective mood is would determine what colors and types of lights are used.

6. All five senses must be engaged to experience God, according to Mark Driscoll.

7. Engaging multiple senses at once will eliminate distractions.

III. Teaching Methods for Volunteers

A. Expository Teaching

1. Expository teaching is defined as the communication of a biblical concept derived from and transmitted through a historical, grammatical, and literary study of a passage in its context. The Holy Spirit first applies this to the personality and experience of the preacher, and then through the preacher applies to the hearers.

2. One reason expository preaching can be effective to those with ADD or ADHD is that it is applicable.

3. Expository teaching is effective because it is culturally relevant to where people live today.

4. It is meant to engage the listener with applications and relation to current culture so that the congregant

remembers the lesson and as a result gleans something from it and grows from it.

B. Multisensory Teaching

1. Multisensory teaching is teaching or communicating that touches on more than just one sense.

2. Multisensory communication stimulates multiple senses: hearing, seeing, touching, and sometimes even smell and taste.

3. Multisensory teaching or communication brings more of the whole person into the teaching process.

4. Learning begins with the senses. They are the gateway to the brain. This is why when it comes to biblical teaching, the senses cannot be ignored. They are vital to learning.

5. Jesus was a multisensory teacher and communicator. Few teachers relied on the power of multisensory teaching more than Jesus.

6. There are three words to remember when presenting or delivering a multisensory lesson: attention, comprehension, and retention.

7. The Bible is paramount in multisensory teaching.

C. One-Point Teaching

  1. One-point teaching strives to present one main idea or concept that the listener will take home.

  2. One-point teaching emphasizes one thing and what to do with that one thing.

  3. Instead of having three, four, or five ideas to present in a lesson, just pick one main idea and build around it.

  4. Instead of having to put together a nice three- or four-point outline with points and subpoints, the teacher or communicator just needs one point, one thought, one concept, and then to build the entire lesson or talk around it, own it and present it.

  5. Make it stick.

IV. Connecting and Coaching as Volunteers

  1. Because of the disorder and the symptoms that go along with the disease, those with ADD or ADHD often struggle in relationships.

  2. Connecting, or building a relationship is a powerful tool for engaging ADD congregants.

3. Ordinary people have the power to change other people's lives.

4. The power to meaningfully change lives depends on connecting, on bringing two people into an experience of shared life.

5. Any volunteer can take time to make a connection.

6. Coaching is a new form of treatment of ADD that is growing in popularity.

7. The increased demand for ADHD coaching comes from the fact that most adults who struggle with ADD or ADHD would like nothing more than to make adjustments that will change their lives for the better.

8. The problem with that is the follow through, which is where coaches can help.

9. The way that coaching works is that there is a coach-patient relationship which is goal driven. The coach actively works with the ADD sufferers to create practical strategies to enhance their lives.

10. Coaching is highly individualized, and for this reason, there is no standard method used by all coaches.

11. Coaching is extremely hands on and is about accountability, which is what those with ADD are showing a desire for.

12. Any volunteer can be a coach. It just takes effort, time, and compassion.

Bibliography

Adeyi, Sam. *Church Volunteers, "God's Workers": God's Volunteers.* Gardners Books, 2007.

"ADD/ADHD Statistics - What Is ADHD? - ADHD." HealthCentral.com - Trusted, Reliable, and Up To Date Health Information. http://www.healthcentral.com/adhd/c/1443/13716/addadhd-statistics (accessed April 1, 2012).

"ADHD and Spiritual Development: Tying It All Together." Church4EveryChild. Building Bridges between Churches and Families of Kids with "Issues." http://drgrcevich.wordpress.com/2010/10/24/adhd-and-spiritual-development-tying-it-all-together/ (accessed April 1, 2012).

"ADHD in Adults: Symptoms, Statistics, Causes, Types, Treatments, and More." WebMD - Better information. Better health. http://www.webmd.com/add-adhd/guide/adhd-adults (accessed April 1, 2012).

Adler, Lenard, and Mari Florence. *Scattered Minds: Hope and Help for Adults with Attention Deficit Hyperactivity Disorder.* New York: G. P. Putnam's Sons, 2006.

"Attention Deficit Hyperactivity Disorder (ADHD): MedlinePlus Medical Encyclopedia." National Library of Medicine - National Institutes of Health. http://www.nlm.nih.gov/medlineplus/ency/article/001551.htm (accessed April 1, 2012).

Barclay, Aileen. "Does Peter Have Attention Deficit Hyperactivity Disorder (ADHD)?" *Journal of Religion, Disability & Health* 12, no. 4 (December 2008): 330–346. SocINDEX with Full Text, EBSCOhost (accessed April 2, 2012).

Bays, Patricia. "The Care and Nurture of Volunteers." *Clergy Journal* 82, no. 7 (May 2006): 8–10. Academic Search Complete, EBSCOhost (accessed April 2, 2012).

Blackwood, Rick. *The Power of Multi-Sensory Preaching and Teaching: Increase Attention, Comprehension, and Retention.* Grand Rapids, MI: Zondervan, 2008.

Burley-Allen, Madelyn. *Listening: The Forgotten Skill.* New York: John Wiley & Sons, 1995.

Carbonell, Mels. *How to Solve the People Puzzle: Understanding Personality Patterns*. Blue Ridge, GA: Uniquely You Resources, 2008.

"CDC - ADHD, Data and Statistics - NCBDDD." Centers for Disease Control and Prevention. http://www.cdc.gov/ncbddd/adhd/data.html (accessed April 1, 2012).

"CDC - ADHD, Prevalence - NCBDDD." Centers for Disease Control and Prevention. http://www.cdc.gov/ncbddd/adhd/prevalence.html (accessed April 1, 2012).

Chapell, Bryan. *Christ-Centered Preaching: Redeeming the Expository Sermon*. Grand Rapids, MI: Baker Books, 1994.

Church, Karin, Charleen M. Gottschalk, and Jane N. Leddy. "20 Ways to ... Enhance Social and Friendship Skills." *Intervention in School and Clinic* 38, no. 5 (May 2003): 307–310. OmniFile Full Text Mega (H. W. Wilson), EBSCOhost (accessed April 2, 2012).

Clancy, Marianne. "Inclusion Identifies the Meaning of Church for a Parent." *Journal of Religion, Disability & Health* 13, no. 3/4 (July 2009): 334–338. SocINDEX with Full Text, EBSCOhost (accessed April 2, 2012).

Coghill, David, and Sarah Seth. "Do the Diagnostic Criteria for ADHD Need to Change? Comments on the Preliminary Proposals of the DSM-5 ADHD and Disruptive Behavior Disorders Committee." *European Child & Adolescent Psychiatry* 20, no. 2 (February 2011): 75–81. CINAHL, EBSCOhost (accessed April 2, 2012).

"Cognitive Behavioral Therapy for Attention Deficit Disorder - Coaching - ADHD." HealthCentral.com - Trusted, Reliable and Up To Date Health Information. http://www.healthcentral.com/adhd/c/8689/124413/cognitive-behavioral/?ic=1112 (accessed April 2, 2012).

"Counseling Services - ADD/ADHD Evaluation and Assessment - Champion Christian Counseling Center, Tomball, Texas." Champion Christian Counseling Center, Tomball, TX. http://www.cccctomball.com/add.html (accessed April 2, 2012).

Crabb, Lawrence J. *Connecting: Healing Ourselves and Our Relationships*. Nashville, TN: W Publishing Group, 2005.

Cummins, Mark D. *Creative Preaching How Multi-Sensory Preaching Connects the Word of God to the Twenty-First Century Culture*. 2004. <http://digitalcommons.liberty.edu/doctoral/372/>.

Davis, Ken. *How to Speak to Youth—and Keep Them Awake at the Same Time.* Grand Rapids, MI: Zondervan, 1996.

Dober, Hans Martin. "What Can the Pastor Learn from Freud? A Historical Perspective on Psychological and Theological Dimensions of Soul Care." *Christian Bioethics: Non-Ecumenical Studies in Medical Morality* 16, no. 1 (January 2010): 61–78. *Academic Search Complete,* EBSCOhost (accessed April 2, 2012).

"Emotional and Behavioral Difficulties and Impairments in Everyday Functioning Among Children with a hHistory of Attention-Deficit/Hyperactivity Disorder [Prev. Chronic Dis. 2006] - PubMed - NCBI." National Center for Biotechnology Information. http://www.ncbi.nlm.nih.gov/sites/entrez?Db=pubmed&Cmd=ShowDetailView&TermToSearch=16539793&log$=activity (accessed April 1, 2012).

Entwistle, David N. *Integrative Approaches to Psychology and Christianity: An Introduction to Worldview Issues, Philosophical Foundations, and Models of Integration.* Eugene, OR: Wipf and Stock Publishers, 2004.

"FASTSTATS - Attention Deficit Hyperactivity Disorder." Centers for Disease Control and Prevention. http://www.cdc.gov/nchs/fastats/adhd.htm (accessed April 1, 2012).

"Frequently Asked Questions about ADHD Medications - Medication - ADHD." HealthCentral.com - Trusted, Reliable and Up To Date Health Information. http://www.healthcentral.com/adhd/c/1443/62998/frequently-medications (accessed April 1, 2012).

Gartner, Stefan. "Staying a Pastor while Talking Like a Psychologist? A Proposal for an Integrative Model." *Christian Bioethics: Non-Ecumenical Studies in Medical Morality* 16, no. 1 (January 2010): 48–60. *Academic Search Complete*, EBSCOhost (accessed April 2, 2012).

Geng, Gretchen. "Investigation of Teachers' Verbal and Non-Verbal Strategies for Managing Attention Deficit Hyperactivity Disorder (ADHD) Students' Behaviours within a Classroom Environment." *Australian Journal of Teacher Education* 36, no. 7 (July 1, 2011): 17–30. ERIC, EBSCOhost (accessed April 2, 2012).

Gerber, Leslie E. "What Child Is This? Christian Parental Virtues and Attention Deficit Hyperactivity Disorder." *Sewanee Theological Review* 50, no. 4 (January 1, 2007): 521–545. ATLA Religion Database, EBSCOhost (accessed April 2, 2012).

Ghanizadeh, A, and N Zarei. "Are GPs Adequately Equipped with the Knowledge for Educating and Counseling of Families with ADHD Children?" *BMC Family Practice* 11, (2010): CINAHL Plus with Full Text, EBSCOhost (accessed April 2, 2012).

Group Publishing. *Special Needs, Special Ministry.* Loveland, CO: Group Pub, 2003.

Halverson, Delia Touchton. *Ready, Set, Teach! Training and Supporting Volunteers in Christian Education.* Nashville, TN: Abingdon Press, 2010.

Halverstadt, Jonathan Scott, and Jerry Seiden. *ADD, Christianity & the Church: A Compassionate Healing Resource to Inform, Inspire, & Illuminate.* Irvine, CA: Spirit of Hope Pub, 2008.

"Harmony Hensley: Welcoming Ministry Environments for Kids with ADHD (Part One) Church4EveryChild." Church4EveryChild Building Bridges between Churches and Families of Kids with "Issues." http://drgrcevich.wordpress.com/2010/10/20/harmony-hensley-welcoming-ministry-environments-for-kids-with-adhd-part-one/ (accessed April 1, 2012).

Hook, J. N., and E. L. Worthington Jr. "Christian Couple Counseling by Professional, Pastoral, and Lay Counselors from a Protestant Perspective: A Nationwide Survey." *American Journal of Family Therapy* 37, no. 2 (March 2009): 169–183. CINAHL Plus with Full Text, EBSCOhost (accessed April 2, 2012).

"How Many Employees Should Your Supervisors Manage? Where Great Workplaces Start." Where Great Workplaces Start Information and Conversation on Everything HR, Brought to You by ERC. http://greatworkplace.wordpress.com/2010/02/17/how-many-employees-should-your-supervisors-manage/ (accessed June 22, 2012).

"How Should a Christian View ADD and ADHD?" Bible Questions Answered. http://www.gotquestions.org/ADD-ADHD-Christian.html (accessed April 1, 2012).

"How to Teach Children with ADHD - ChurchLeaders.com - Christian Leadership Blogs, Articles, Videos, How To's, and Free Resources." ChurchLeaders.com - Christian Leadership Blogs, Articles, Videos, How To's, and Free Resources. http://www.churchleaders.com/children/childrens-ministry-how-tos/157672-how-to-teach-children-with-adhd.html (accessed April 1, 2012).

Humphrey, Neil. "Including Students with Attention-Deficit/Hyperactivity Disorder in Mainstream Schools." *British Journal of Special Education* 36, no. 1 (March 2009): 19–25. *Academic Search Complete*, EBSCOhost (accessed April 2, 2012).

Hybels, Bill. *The Volunteer Revolution: Unleashing the Power of Everybody*. Grand Rapids, MI: Zondervan, 2004.

Johnson, Jacob J. "Attention-Deficit/Hyperactivity Disorders among Students in Christian Colleges and Universities." *Christian Higher Education* 10, no. 1 (January 1, 2011): 57–70. ERIC, EBSCOhost (accessed April 2, 2012).

Kelley, Susan D. M., William English, and Pat Schwallie-Gaddis. "Exemplary Counseling Strategies for Developmental Transitions of Young Women with Attention Deficit/Hyperactivity Disorder." *Journal of Counseling and Development* 85, no. 2 (April 15, 2007): 173–181. OmniFile Full Text Mega (H. W. Wilson), EBSCOhost (accessed April 2, 2012).

Kimball, Dan, and Lilly Lewin. *Sacred Space: A Hands-On Guide to Creating Multisensory Worship Experiences for Youth Ministry*. Grand Rapids, MI: Youth Specialties, 2008.

Kinnaman, David, and Aly Hawkins. *You Lost Me: Why Young Christians Are Leaving Church—and Rethinking Faith*. Grand Rapids, MI: Baker Books, 2011.

Lovell, George, and Neil Richardson. *Sustaining Preachers and Preaching: A Practical Guide*. London: T & T Clark, 2011.

Miller, Kim. *Handbook for Multi-Sensory Worship*. Nashville, TN: Abingdon Press, 1999.

Morgan, Tony, and Tim Stevens. *Simply Strategic Volunteers: Empowering People for Ministry*. Loveland, CO: Group, 2005.

"Multisensory Worship." Wikipedia. en.wikipedia.org/wiki/Multisensory_worship (accessed April 2, 2012).

"Myth: ADHD Is a Childhood Disorder - ADHD in Adults - ADHD." HealthCentral.com - Trusted, Reliable and Up To Date Health Information. http://www.healthcentral.com/adhd/c/1443/11092/myth-adhd-disorder/?ic=1112 (accessed April 1, 2012).

"Myth: ADHD Cannot Be Accurately Diagnosed - ADHD Tests - ADHD." HealthCentral.com - Trusted, Reliable and Up To Date Health Information. http://www.healthcentral.com/adhd/c/1443/14462/myth-adhd-diagnosed/?ic=1112 (accessed April 1, 2012).

Neff, Blake J. A. *Pastor's Guide to Interpersonal Communication: The Other Six Days*. New York: Haworth Pastoral Press, 2006.

Nelson, Paul. "Church Aims to Make Service Comfortable: Bridge Christian Provides Short Sermons, Theatrical Worship and Relaxing Atmosphere." *Times Union* (Albany, NY) (February 21, 2007): Newspaper Source Plus, EBSCOhost (accessed April 2, 2012).

"Parenting a Child with ADHD: Helping Your Child." WebMD - Better information. Better health. http://www.webmd.com/add-adhd/features/6-parenting-tips-for-raising-kids-with-adhd (accessed April 1, 2012).

Petersen, Jim. *Why Don't We Listen Better? Communicating & Connecting in Relationships*. Tigard, OR: Petersen Publications, 2007.

Petri, Gary A. *The Proper Care and Feeding of Church Volunteers: A Practical Guide for Volunteer Leaders*. Kansas City: Sheed & Ward, 1996.

Powell, Kara Eckmann, and Chap Clark. *Sticky Faith: Everyday Ideas to Build Lasting Faith in Your Kids*. Grand Rapids, MI: Zondervan, 2011.

Rainer, Thom S., and Sam S. Rainer. *Essential Church? Reclaiming a Generation of Dropouts.* Nashville, TN: B & H Books, 2008.

Rapada, Amy. *The Special Needs Ministry Handbook: A Church's Guide to Reaching Children with Disabilities and Their Families.* CGR Publishing, 2007.

Richards, Larry. *Creative Bible Teaching.* Chicago: Moody Press, 1973.

Robinson, Haddon W. *Biblical Preaching: The Development and Delivery of Expository Messages.* Grand Rapids, MI: Baker Book House, 1980.

Schultz, Richard L. "For I Did Not Shrink from Declaring to You the Whole Purpose of God: Biblical Theology's Role within Christian Counseling." *Edification: The Transdisciplinary Journal of Christian Psychology* 4, no. 1 (May 2010): 47–55. *Academic Search Complete*, EBSCOhost (accessed April 2, 2012).

Stanley, Andy. *The Next Generation Leader: 5 Essentials for Those Who Will Shape the Future.* Sisters, OR: Multnomah, 2003.

Stanley, Andy, and Ed Young. *Can We Do That? 24 Innovative Practices That Will Change the Way You Do Church.* West Monroe, LA: Howard Pub, 2002.

Stanley, Andy, Reggie Joiner, and Lane Jones. *7 Practices of Effective Ministry*. Sisters, OR: Multnomah Publishers, 2004.

Stanley, Andy, and Lane Jones. *Communicating for a Change*. Sisters, OR: Multnomah Publishers, 2006.

Stanley, Andy. *Making Vision Stick*. Grand Rapids, MI: Zondervan, 2007.

"Statistics about ADD in Adults & Children | ADDitude - Adults & Children with ADD ADHD." Attention Deficit Disorder | ADHD Symptoms, Medication, Treatment, Diagnosis, Parenting ADD Children and More: Information from ADDitude. http://www.additudemag.com/adhd/article/688.html (accessed April 1, 2012).

Stevenson, Dwight E., and Charles F. Diehl. *Reaching People from the Pulpit: A Guide to Effective Sermon Delivery*. New York: Harper, 1958.

Stewart, John Robert. *Bridges Not Walls: A Book about Interpersonal Communication*. New York: McGraw-Hill, 1990.

Stewart, Teena M. "Training, Equipping, and Coaching." *Clergy Journal* 79, no. 8 (July 2003): 23–24. *Academic Search Complete*, EBSCOhost (accessed April 2, 2012).

Scott Sullender, R. "Perspectives from the Second Generation of Pastoral Counselors." *Pastoral Psychology* 60, no. 5 (October 2011): 751–754. *Academic Search Complete*, EBSCOhost (accessed April 2, 2012).

"The Internet, Short Attention Spans, and Preaching | Worship, Music, Culture, Aesthetics - Religious Affections Ministries." Worship, Music, Culture, and Aesthetics - Religious Affections Ministries. http://religiousaffections.org/articles/articles-on-church/the-internet-short-attention-spans-and-preaching/ (accessed April 1, 2012).

Towns, Elmer L., and Ed Stetzer. *Perimeters of Light: Biblical Boundaries for the Emerging Church*. Chicago: Moody Publishers, 2004.

"Treating Adult ADHD." WebMD - Better information. Better health. http://www.webmd.com/add-adhd/features/adult-adhd-treatment (accessed April 1, 2012).

Vaughan, Brigette S., Holly J. Roberts, and Howard Needelman. "Current Medications for the Treatment of Attention-Deficit/Hyperactivity Disorder." *Psychology in the Schools* 46, no. 9 (November 1, 2009): 846–856. ERIC, EBSCOhost (accessed April 2, 2012).

Vernon, David, Ann Frick, and John Gruzelier. "Neurofeedback as a Treatment for ADHD: A Methodological Review with Implications for Future Research." *Journal of Neurotherapy* 8, no. 2 (June 2004): 53–82. Academic Search Complete, EBSCOhost (accessed April 2, 2012).

Wadsworth, John S., and Dennis C. Harper. "Adults with Attention-Deficit/Hyperactivity Disorder: Assessment and Treatment Strategies." *Journal of Counseling and Development* 85, no. 1 (December 15, 2007): 101–109. OmniFile Full Text Mega (H. W. Wilson), EBSCOhost (accessed April 2, 2012).

Wallace, Sue. *Multi-Sensory Church: Over 30 Innovative Ready-to-Use Ideas*. Milton Keynes: Scripture Union, 2002.

Welch, Edward T. "Understanding and Helping Those with Attention Deficit Disorder-FamilyLife.com." Help and Hope for Marriages and Families-FamilyLife.com. http://www.familylife.com/site/c.dnJHKLNnFoG/b.6175085/k.C834/Understanding_and_Helping_Those_with_Attention_Deficit_Disorder.htm (accessed April 1, 2012).

White, Joe, and Jim Weidmann. *Parents' Guide to the Spiritual Mentoring of Teens*. Wheaton, IL: Tyndale House Publishers, 2001.

Wicks, Robert J., and Tina C. Buck. "Reframing for Change: The Use of Cognitive Behavioral Therapy and Native Psychology in Pastoral Ministry and Formation." *Human Development* 32, no. 3 (Fall 2011): 8-14. Education Research Complete, EBSCOhost (accessed April 2, 2012).

Winfrey, David. "Biblical Therapy." *Christian Century* 124, no. 2 (January 23, 2007): 24. MasterFILE Premier, EBSCOhost (accessed April 2, 2012).

Yount, William R. *Created to Learn*. Nashville, TN: B & H Academic, 2010.